Healthy, Quick & Easy
BENTO BOX

Healthy, Quick & Easy
BENTO BOX

Ophelia Chien

DK

Publisher Mike Sanders
Editor Ann Barton
Designer and Art Director Rebecca Batchelor
Photographer Kelley Schuyler
Food Stylist Lovoni Walker
Chef Ashley Brooks
Recipe Tester Julie Harrington
Proofreaders Lisa Starnes, Monica Stone
Indexer Brad Herriman

First American Edition, 2021
Published in the United States by DK Publishing
6081 E. 82nd Street, Indianapolis, IN 46250

Copyright © 2021 by Chia Huei Chien
21 22 23 24 25 10 9 8 7 6 5 4 3 2 1
001-322098-JUL2021

Library of Congress Catalog Number: 2020950751
ISBN: 978-1-6156-4993-8

DK books are available at special discounts when purchased
in bulk for sales promotions, premiums, fund-raising,
or educational use. For details, contact:
SpecialSales@dk.com

Printed and bound in China

For the curious

www.dk.com

For my grandmother Peach Song,
who brought me love and creativity

CONTENTS

Pan-Seared Salmon (page 33)

Rose Gyoza (page 71)

INTRODUCTION

When I was in middle school, my favorite time of the day was lunch break. Once I opened my steaming hot bento box, the tedious school work and academic pressures faded away. The world was simple and vibrant for me while I enjoyed my tiny feast. I love the tidiness of bento. Each neatly arranged dish has a distinctive flavor, yet together they present a course of harmony.

Growing up in Taiwan means living with a vigorous fusion food culture. Dishes and flavors from various cuisines are often found in daily bento box lunches, even though most of them have a twist from local ingredients. This versatile attitude toward food inspired me when I started cooking in the United States. Back then, I was just a student who neither knew about Asian grocery stores nor owned a car. The limitations imposed by a lack of familiar ingredients, equipment, and time opened up another door for my cooking style. I have found so much pleasure using fresh produce and simple spices that are common here to recreate the flavors that were once dear to me.

Without compromising the taste, I simplified the cooking process of my recipes to make meal prep possible in my daily life. The other benefit of doing so is the food turns out to be healthy. I believe that the essence of cooking is to bring out the best flavor of each ingredient with a minimum of additives, so I limit the use of processed ingredients and sugar in my bento creations. On top of that, the greatest joy I have found in making bento is designing the presentation of the box. When I conceive of an idea for bento, I consider the structure, flavors, and colors of the whole box. As a result, all the bento boxes in this book are designed to be enjoyable to the palate as well as to the eye.

I sincerely hope that the array of cuisines reflected in this book will help you to discover how adaptable bento can be and to master the easy but delicious seasoning skills that I have carefully curated. Whether you picked up this book intending to expand your everyday menus or just to browse for inspiration, my wish is for you to find interesting alternatives to your daily meals and to start your own culinary adventure from here.

BENTO
BASICS

ABOUT BENTO

The concept of bento originated in Japan. The word **bento** means "convenient," and it is used to refer to the a convenient packed lunch for work, travel, or picnicking. The tradition of preparing these carefully packed lunches dates back hundreds of years. At first, Japanese bento consisted of simple dried rice balls with pickles, but over time, bento has evolved into many delicious forms and has become an integral part of lunch culture. Bento is also popular in other Asian countries including Taiwan, Korea, China, the Philippines, Thailand, and India, all of which have their unique lunch box culture. These lunch boxes usually include rice as staple food along with side dishes rooted in local cuisine. They are prepared for both kids and adults, usually for lunch but also for dinner.

Bento remains a popular tradition that many people practice daily. Traditionally, people made bento for their families or loved ones both as a way of care giving and as a way to economize. Opening a thoughtfully prepared and beautifully arranged lunch box is like opening a gift. It makes a daily meal a little more special and eliminates the need to go out for lunch. Now, people may choose to make bento for different reasons, such as to pursue a healthy diet, to cut down on snacks, to maintain an ecofriendly lifestyle, or as a hobby. No matter what your reasons are, the process of preparing bento is a form of self-care and brings mindfulness to cooking and eating.

ABOUT THIS BOOK

Making bento should be casual and creative, just as it has always been in home kitchens around the world. This book includes instructions for 30 bento box meals. Each bento consists of three to four simple dishes that are easy to prepare. One third of the bento recipes in this book are based on traditional Japanese flavors and cooking techniques; one third of the recipes are inspired by other Asian cuisines; and one third of the recipes are based on traditionally Western flavors and ingredients. The majority of the ingredients used in these recipes are available from regular grocery stores, although you may need to visit the international aisle.

BENTO COMPONENTS

While "bento-style" lunch boxes with individual compartments have increasingly come to represent bento in the Western imagination, this type of box is not required to prepare bento, nor is it exclusively representative of bento preparation in Japan or other Asian countries with robust bento cultures. The bento in this book utilize traditional packing techniques to keep foods separate, but you can use divided bento boxes if you prefer. Each bento has three components.

MAIN DISH

The main dish is the central dish of each box, and it usually includes the primary source of protein in the meal. While most bento boxes include meat, some are vegetarian or can easily be adapted to omit meat.

SIDE DISHES

The main dish is accompanied by one to three simple side dishes. These are often vegetable-based dishes that add color and complement the flavors of the main dish. However, you can mix and match side dishes according to your tastes to build your own bento creations.

STAPLE

Traditionally, white rice is the base, or staple dish, around which the bento is built. Many of the bento boxes in this book include rice, but some rely on another starch such as pasta or bread. You can use the suggested staple, swap in another, or omit the staple entirely. Preparation instructions for staples can be found on pages 152 to 155.

To help you plan your meal preparation, each recipe includes suggested storage methods, shelf life, and number of servings. Most recipes make four servings, which can be dinner for two right after the food is made and two packed lunches for the next day. Recipes that require a longer preparation time may have larger serving sizes and a longer shelf life because making a big batch is more efficient. You can adjust the serving sizes as needed, and use these recipes according to your meal plan for the coming days.

BALANCED NUTRITION

One of the benefits of bento-style meals is that they are preportioned, making it easy to control portion size. Each bento in this book contains fewer than 500 calories and provides a balanced meal. None of the recipes require deep-frying, and the goal is to bring out the natural flavors of each ingredient with a minimum of seasoning and more importantly, without using artificial flavors or food additives.

KITCHEN EQUIPMENT

The bento dishes in this book do not require special equipment or cookware. You will only need a **sharp knife**, a **vegetable peeler**, a **spatula**, a **baking sheet**, a **saucepan**, and a **skillet**, which can be nonstick, cast iron, or stainless steel. If you use a stainless steel or cast-iron skillet, be sure that the pan and oil are properly heated before you start cooking. You may need a little extra oil on these surfaces to prevent sticking.

While not essential, there are some specialized pieces of equipment that can be very useful. A **rice cooker** or **multicooker,** such as an Instant Pot, can help you make rice effortlessly and prepare stewed dishes in a remarkably short period of time. Also, a nonstick **Japanese omelet (tamagoyaki) pan** is the best pan for making traditional egg rolls (rolled omelets). It is much easier to achieve the rolled shape using one of these small, rectangular pans than it is using a round frying pan.

Tamagoyaki pan + spatula

CHOOSING YOUR BENTO BOX

Bento boxes come in an array of designs and materials. They may be made of plastic, metal, or bamboo and may include one or two tiers. Look for a box that fits your budget and appeals to your aesthetic and lifestyle. Generally, a leakproof, lightweight, and microwavable bento box can satisfy most needs of people. Things to consider:

- Do you heat your bento?

- How much do you want to eat?

- How will you be transporting your bento box?

- What kinds of foods do you plan to pack in your bento box?

Some bento boxes are made with compartments or come with removable dividers to prevent flavors from mingling and individual dishes from moving around during transportation. If you frequently make bento dishes with more liquid, like stews or curries, you may consider getting this style of bento box. However, if you simply want to keep dishes separate to avoid mixing flavors, you can use lettuce, rice, or silicone baking cups to keep dishes from mingling.

INGREDIENTS

The majority of the ingredients used in these bento recipes can be found in your pantry or local grocery store. There are a few specialty ingredients that you might need to source from an Asian grocery store, but in most cases, you will be able to find what you need in the international foods aisle of any grocery store.

BENTO PREP TIPS

As with any cooking endeavor, making bento is easiest when you plan ahead and maximize your prep time. When you can, prep ahead and prepare foods in batches to make your bento assembly as quick and easy as possible.

PREP AHEAD

To save time, you can prepare multiple bento meals at once or prep portions of dishes in advance. Slicing, marinating, and freezing meat in advance makes it easy to thaw and cook. Vegetables and rice can be prepared ahead and frozen or used throughout the week.

MEAT

Slicing meat: Purchase precut meat when possible. If you are preparing multiple bento meals at once, cut all the meat at the same time. To thinly slice meat, seal the meat in a plastic bag and place on a tray. Freeze for 90 minutes. This will make the meat firm enough to slice cleanly. Using a very sharp knife, slice the meat against the grain into ⅛-inch (0.3cm) slices. If the meat is too soft to slice, return it to the freezer for 10 minutes .

Marinating meat: Meat dishes that require marinating can be prepped ahead of time and frozen. This extends the shelf life and also saves time when you're ready to cook. Meat generally becomes softer and juicier after marinating, especially chicken breasts!

Thawing meat: Thaw the meat or seafood that you need 3 to 5 hours in advance to make sure that it's completely back at room temperature.

VEGETABLES

Many side dishes call for blanched vegetables, which are cooked quickly in boiling water. To cut down on prep time, blanch multiple batches of vegetables at once and freeze them. Vegetables like cauliflower, broccoli, beans, and carrots can be frozen for months and quickly thawed.

RICE

Rice can be prepared ahead of time and refrigerated for up to 3 days or frozen. Store cooked rice in airtight containers and seal them immediately to prevent the rice from drying out. Before reheating, fluff the rice with a spoon, and use a spray bottle to mist the rice with water. Microwave for 1 to 2 minutes with a food cover.

To freeze, package cooked rice in freezer-safe plastic bags, removing as much air as possible. To reheat, remove the rice from the bag and microwave for 2 to 3 minutes with a food cover.

COOK EFFICIENTLY

Make the most of your time in the kitchen by using efficient cooking techniques.

Read the recipes first. Read each recipe so you know what to expect. Start with the recipe that has the longest preparation time. You can often begin making rice or marinating meat before moving on to the next steps.

Clean and cut all ingredients together. Have all ingredients washed, chopped, and measured before you begin cooking. This ensures a tidy work surface and makes it easier to follow the recipe without distraction.

Use one pan to minimize dishes. If you're cooking only for bento and meal preparation, start with the dish that has the lightest flavor—usually vegetables, egg, and then meat. This way, you don't need to wash the pan in between dishes. Use a paper towel to wipe out any excess grease and rinse with hot water to remove residue. However, if you're cooking for a meal and for bento, start with the meat, then the egg, and lastly vegetables. This way, all foods can remain hot when you finish cooking.

Cook first and assemble later. Bento boxes are meant to be assembled on the day they are eaten or the night before. However, this doesn't mean you can't prep ahead. To keep the flavor and texture of each dish intact, store each dish separately in a clean, dry container, and label it with the recipe name and expiration date. Assemble your bento the day you plan to eat it or the night before.

Make ahead and freeze. Some meat and root vegetable dishes, especially stews, take a long time to make and make large quantities. In this case, you can make them ahead and freeze them in small portions.

BENTO ASSEMBLY

Bento are meant to be balanced meals, as well as appealing to the eye. Attention to arrangement and consideration for aesthetics show that the meal was thoughtfully prepared.

PROPER PROPORTIONS

Before you begin packing your bento, first plan the food portions of your bento boxes. A bento typically consists of three main sections: staple (rice), protein, and vegetable. The staple is usually some form of rice but could also be quinoa, pasta, or other starchy food.

Most of the recipes in this book are designed to have ⅓ staple, ⅓ protein, and ⅓ vegetable, but sometimes they have ¼ staple, ¼ protein, and ½ vegetable. You can adjust the proportions to suit your nutritional needs.

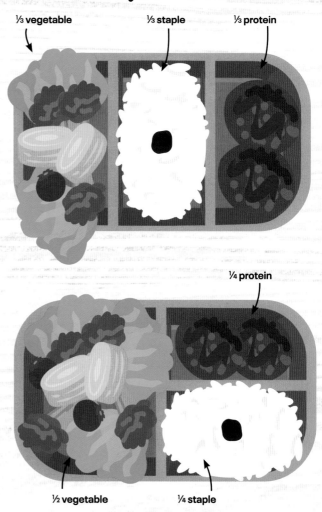

⅓ **vegetable** ⅓ **staple** ⅓ **protein**

¼ **protein**

½ **vegetable** ¼ **staple**

When packing bento, aim for balanced portions of staple, protein, and vegetable.

PLEASING PRESENTATION

white

purple

yellow

red

green

Bento are meant to be visually appealing as well as delicious. The color and arrangement of the food contribute to the enjoyment of the meal. Traditionally, Japanese bento include the following five colors: white, red, green, yellow (or orange), and black (or dark purple). The bento boxes in this book are all designed to include at least four different colors to make them look appealing. If you plan to design your own bento, don't forget to consider the colors of each dish. Place dishes with contrasting colors next to one another to make the overall presentation vibrant and colorful.

When packing bento, place all dishes tightly and arrange the food neatly. Tight, tidy arrangements can prevent the dishes from being tossed around in transportation and also make the bento look beautiful. If possible, always have some lettuce, cherry tomatoes, and cucumbers in your fridge. These vegetables can be used to create dividers and fill gaps, and they also add a pop of color and visual appeal.

Make It Colorful!

Garnishes are a great way to add color to your bento. Keep a few of these simple garnishes on hand to add the finishing touch.

Cherry tomatoes
Fresh herbs
Furikake
Lemon slices
Lettuce leaves
Nori sheets (can be cut into patterns)

Radishes
Sesame seeds (black and white)
Umeboshi (salted Japanese plums)

PACKING YOUR BENTO

Once you have prepared your dishes, pack your bento following four simple steps.

1 Pack the rice (or other staple).

Use a spoon or spatula to scoop the desired amount of rice into your bento box. You can place the rice in one corner of the box or spread it flat as the bottom layer of the whole bento. If you feel playful, you can also make rice balls with fillings that you like. Medium- or short-grain white rice varieties are best for creating rice balls; they are glutenous and will hold together more easily than long-grain varieties.

2 Pack the side dishes.

On the opposite side of the bento box from the rice, pack the side dishes, like vegetables and egg rolls. For dishes with stronger flavors, use lettuce leaves, parchment paper, or silicone baking cups to create compartments. If your bento includes cold side dishes, place them on lettuce leaves or in silicone baking cups so they can be removed easily before reheating the bento box. When packing stew or curry, you can pack rice in the middle of the bento box to create a barrier to separate the curry from other dishes. Take care with foods like turmeric and beets that may leave stains on your bento box. To be safe, you can line the box with a sheet of parchment paper to prevent staining.

3 Pack the main dish.

After the rice and side dishes are packed, place the main dish either on top of the rice or in the middle of the box. If the main dish has a crispy exterior and you don't want the moisture from the rice to soften it, you can place the main dish on a lettuce leaf.

4 Final check and garnish.

After all the dishes are placed into the bento box, add some garnishing pieces for visual appeal and flavor. Garnishes are optional, but they are a simple way to elevate your bento with added color and texture. Make sure that the whole bento is packed tightly and fully so that the food won't be tossed around in transportation. If there are any gaps, fill them in with additional lettuce leaves or other garnish.

1

2

3

4

STORAGE AND REHEATING

STORAGE

The individual components of each bento box can be made ahead and stored before assembly, either in the refrigerator or freezer. For the best flavor and texture, assemble your bento box the night before you plan to eat it or in the morning. Assembled bento can then be refrigerated for up to 24 hours.

SERVING TEMPERATURE

Each bento recipe includes a recommended serving temperature of hot, warm, or cold.

Hot: heat right before eating.

Warm: heat 3 to 4 hours before eating.

Cold: no heating required. Eat at room temperature.

Most of the bento recipes in this book taste best when served hot or warm. You can decide which serving temperature works best for you depending on your preference, the availability of heating devices, and convenience. Bento meals that are meant to be served cold can be left at room temperature or made ahead a few hours before eating.

HEATING BENTO

Bento meals can be easily reheated in the microwave as long as your bento box is made of a microwave-safe material. Glass, ceramic, plastic, and silicone bento boxes are generally microwave safe. Wood and metal bento boxes should not be placed in the microwave.

1. **Remove cold dishes.** Before heating, remove any side dishes that do not need to be heated, such as salads or pickles, and place them on the bento lid.

2. **Mist with water.** For better flavor and texture, use a spray bottle to lightly mist the food with water. This counteracts the drying effects of reheating. Spray 5 to 6 times evenly on the whole box and 3 to 4 more times on the rice to add moisture.

3. **Place microwave cover over food.** Covering the bento with a microwave-safe food cover will prevent the food from splattering and create a steaming effect while heating the bento.

4. **Reheat!** Most bento meals will need about 90 seconds to 2 minutes on high to reheat.

Omusubi

TRADITIONAL JAPANESE BENTO

ROASTED MACKEREL
WITH MISO VEGETABLE STIR-FRY AND SWEET JAPANESE PUMPKIN

This classic Japanese bento includes delicious, crisp-skinned roasted mackerel paired with an umami-rich medley of colorful vegetables.

NUTRITION PER BOX

335 calories
Total fat 12g
Cholesterol 49mg
Sodium 759mg
Total carb 35g
Protein 20g

COMPONENTS

MAIN DISH	Roasted Mackerel (page 30)
SIDE DISHES	Miso Vegetable Stir-Fry (page 31)
	Sweet Japanese Pumpkin (page 31)
STAPLE	Jasmine Rice (page 153; 1/3 cup per serving)
GARNISH	watermelon radish

SERVING TEMPERATURE: warm or cold

MAIN DISH
ROASTED MACKEREL

 4 SERVINGS   10 MIN   20 MIN

STORAGE: **Refrigerate up to 3 days.**

2 mackerel fillets
with skin, about 5oz
(140g) each

¼ tsp salt

4 lemon wedges

1 Preheat the oven to 425°F (220°C).

2 Rinse the mackerel fillets and pat dry with paper towels. Sprinkle salt on both sides of the fillets. Let sit for 5 minutes. Use paper towels to remove the excess water from the surface of the fish.

3 Place the fish on a baking sheet skin side up and roast for 16 minutes. Cut each fillet in half, and remove any visible bones before packing them into bento boxes. Add a lemon wedge to each box, and squeeze lemon juice over the fish before eating.

SIDE DISHES
MISO VEGETABLE STIR-FRY

 4 SERVINGS 10 MIN 15 MIN

STORAGE: **Refrigerate up to 3 days.**

1 tbsp red miso paste

1 tsp mirin

1 tsp soy sauce

1 tsp water

1½ tsp vegetable oil

1 red bell pepper, cut into bite-sized pieces

1 head of broccoli or Romanesco, cut into florets

½ head of cauliflower, cut into florets

2 chikuwa (optional), cut into bite-sized pieces

1. In a small bowl, whisk together the miso, mirin, soy sauce, and water until the miso is fully dissolved.

2. In a large skillet, heat the oil over medium heat. When hot, add the bell pepper, broccoli, and cauliflower. Cook for 2 minutes or until the vegetables are bright in color but still crisp. Add the chikuwa, if using, and pour in the miso mixture. Mix the vegetables with the sauce and cover. Cook, covered, for 3 to 5 minutes or until the vegetables are tender-crisp.

SWEET JAPANESE PUMPKIN

 4 SERVINGS 10 MIN 20 MIN

STORAGE: **Refrigerate up to 4 days with sauce.**

½ kabocha squash (Japanese pumpkin)

1½ tbsp soy sauce

1½ tbsp mirin

1 tsp cooking sake

¼ tsp bonito stock powder, such as Hondashi

1½-2 cups water

1. Remove the seeds from the squash and cut it into bite-sized pieces (no need to peel). If the squash is too hard to cut, place it in the microwave on high for 2 minutes to soften it.

2. To a large saucepan or pot, add the squash and all remaining ingredients. The water should not quite cover the squash. Cover and bring to a boil over medium heat. Once boiling, reduce heat to medium-low. Simmer for 10 minutes, stirring occasionally to keep the squash covered with sauce. When a fork can easily pierce the squash, it is done. Refrigerate until ready to assemble the bento.

PAN-SEARED SALMON
WITH PORK ROLL-UPS
AND CARROT EGG ROLL

Crispy golden-skinned salmon is paired with two delicate, bite-sized side dishes in this striking and colorful bento box.

NUTRITION PER BOX

409 calories
Total fat 23g
Cholesterol 194mg
Sodium 465mg
Total carb 23g
Protein 26g

COMPONENTS

MAIN DISH	Pan-Seared Salmon (page 34)
SIDE DISHES	Pork Roll-Ups (page 35) Carrot Egg Roll (page 35)
STAPLE	Jasmine Rice (page 153; ⅓ cup per serving)
GARNISH	radish, cucumber slices

SERVING TEMPERATURE: warm or cold

MAIN DISH
PAN-SEARED SALMON

 4 SERVINGS   5 MIN   15 MIN

STORAGE: **Refrigerate up to 3 days.**

2 salmon fillets with skin, about 5oz (140g) each

Salt, to taste

2 tbsp all-purpose flour

1 tsp vegetable oil

Freshly ground black pepper, to taste

Lemon wedges (optional), to serve

1 Pat the salmon dry with paper towels. Sprinkle salt on both sides of the salmon, and then coat the salmon with a thin layer of flour.

2 Pat the salmon gently to remove any excess flour. In a large nonstick skillet, heat the vegetable oil over medium heat. When hot, place the salmon in the pan, skin side down. Cook for 3 minutes on each side. (If the thickness of the fillets is greater than ½ inch [1.5cm], cook for 4 minutes on each side.)

3 Cut each piece of salmon in half before packing in bento boxes. Just before serving, sprinkle with a pinch of pepper and a squeeze of lemon, if using.

SIDE DISHES
PORK ROLL-UPS

 4 SERVINGS 10 MIN 10 MIN

STORAGE: **Refrigerate up to 3 days.**

8 long, straight green beans

8 carrot sticks, cut to the width and length of the beans

Pinch of salt

4–8 slices pork belly or bacon, very thinly sliced

1 tsp vegetable oil

1 Place the green beans and carrots in a small microwave-safe dish and sprinkle with salt. Microwave on high for 60 seconds until slightly softened.

2 Place 2 beans and 2 carrots together on 1 slice of pork belly. Roll them up. If the pork slices are too narrow, layer 2 slices.

3 In a large nonstick skillet, heat the vegetable oil over medium heat. When hot, place the rolls in the pan, seam side down, and cook for 1 minute to set. After the rolls are set, use tongs or chopsticks to turn the rolls, allowing them to brown on all sides. Remove from the pan and let cool for 2 to 3 minutes before cutting into bite-sized pieces.

CARROT EGG ROLL

 4 SERVINGS 3 MIN 15 MIN

STORAGE: **Refrigerate up to 3 days.**

½ cup grated carrot

3 large eggs

1 tsp mayonnaise

Pinch of salt

1 tsp vegetable oil

1 In a medium bowl, whisk together the carrot, eggs, mayonnaise, and salt until well combined. In a tamagoyaki pan or small nonstick skillet, heat the oil over low heat.

2 Add half of the egg mixture to the pan. Cook without stirring for 3 minutes or until the bottom is set but the top is still a bit runny.

3 Using a spatula, gently roll up the egg, starting at the edge opposite the handle and rolling toward the handle. Push the rolled egg to the side of the pan opposite the handle.

4 Pour the remaining egg mixture into the pan. Using a spatula, lift the rolled egg so it can be coated with a new layer of egg mixture. Repeat step 3, rolling the egg toward the handle. Remove from the heat and let the completed egg roll rest for 3 minutes in the pan before slicing.

HONEY GINGER BEEF
WITH HARD-BOILED EGG, PICKLED ONION, AND BROCCOLI

Thinly sliced beef is marinated in a sweet and savory sauce and paired with vibrant vegetables in this bright and beautiful bento. The meat can be easily prepped ahead.

NUTRITION PER BOX

459 calories
Total fat 18g
Cholesterol 250mg
Sodium 1,044mg
Total carb 45g
Protein 29g

COMPONENTS

MAIN DISH	Honey Ginger Beef (page 38)
SIDE DISHES	Hard-Boiled Eggs (page 38) Pickled Onion (page 39) Broccoli (page 39)
STAPLE	Purple Rice (page 154; ⅓ cup per serving)
GARNISH	cherry tomato, sesame seeds

SERVING TEMPERATURE:
hot or warm

MAIN DISH
HONEY GINGER BEEF

 4 SERVINGS

 15 MIN

 10 MIN

STORAGE: Refrigerate up to 3 days; freeze up to 15 days.

2 tbsp honey

2 tbsp grated fresh ginger

10oz (280g) skirt steak, thinly sliced; or flank steak, chuck steak, or rib eye

2 tsp vegetable oil

½ yellow onion, thinly sliced

2 tbsp cooking sake

2 tbsp mirin

3 tbsp soy sauce

6 tbsp dashi (Japanese stock) or water

1 tsp potato starch or corn starch (optional)

2 tsp water (optional)

Pinch of chili powder (optional)

1   To a medium bowl, add the honey, ginger, and beef, turning to coat fully. Marinate for 5 to 10 minutes.

2   In a large nonstick skillet, heat the oil over medium-high heat. Add the onion, and cook for 2 minutes or until soft. Add the marinated beef. Cook for 2 minutes more.

3   Add the sake, mirin, soy sauce, and dashi. Bring to a boil. Reduce the heat, and simmer for 2 to 3 minutes. For a thicker sauce, mix the starch and water in a small bowl and add to the pan. Stir for 1 minute or until the sauce thickens.

4   For added spice, sprinkle with chili powder before serving.

SIDE DISHES
HARD-BOILED EGGS

4 eggs

 8 SERVINGS   1 MIN   10 MIN

STORAGE: Refrigerate up to 4 days.

1   Place the eggs in a small saucepan. Add water to cover by ½ inch (1cm).

2   Bring to a boil over medium-high heat. Stir occasionally while cooking. When boiling, remove from heat and cover. Let sit for 4 to 5 minutes.

3   Transfer the eggs to a bowl of ice water to cool. When cool, refrigerate until ready to assemble bento. Peel and halve just before assembling.

PICKLED ONION

 8 SERVINGS   5 MIN   NONE

STORAGE: **Refrigerate up to 2 months.**

1½ cups thinly sliced red onion (about ½ onion)

1 tsp freshly squeezed lemon juice

2 tbsp granulated sugar

Pinch of salt

Rice vinegar or apple cider vinegar

Water

1 Soak the onion in a bowl of ice water for 5 minutes, and then drain the onion to remove excess water.

2 In a clean pint-size jar, combine the lemon juice, sugar, and salt. Add the onion, and pour in vinegar until it covers half of the onion. Then, add water until the onion is fully covered.

3 Marinate for at least 2 hours before serving. Marinate up to 4 hours for a tender texture. Pickled onion can be stored in the refrigerator for up to 2 months.

BROCCOLI

 8 SERVINGS   5 MIN   5 MIN

STORAGE: **Refrigerate up to 4 days; freeze up to 15 days.**

2 broccoli crowns, cut into bite-sized pieces

Meat from 1-2 snow crab legs or imitation crab sticks, torn into pieces (optional)

1 tsp olive oil (optional)

Salt and freshly ground black pepper, to taste

1 In a medium saucepan, bring 4 to 5 cups of salted water to a boil over high heat. Add the broccoli. When the water begins to boil again, remove from the heat. (Alternatively, you can microwave the broccoli with 1 cup of salted water for 2–3 minutes.)

2 Drain the broccoli and put in a medium bowl. Add the crab and olive oil, if using, and toss with salt and pepper.

PORK ONION RINGS
WITH BELL PEPPER FRITTATA
AND SAUTÉED ZUCCHINI

This bento packs a surprise with a juicy onion filling inside the pork ring. Nibble with some frittata, zucchini, and squash, and enjoy the natural sweetness from the vegetables.

475 calories
Total fat 17g
Cholesterol 282mg
Sodium 830mg
Total carb 51g
Protein 28g

COMPONENTS

MAIN DISH Pork Onion Rings (page 42)

SIDE DISHES Bell Pepper Frittata (page 43)
Sautéed Zucchini (page 43)

STAPLE Jasmine Rice (page 153; 1/3 cup per serving)

GARNISH umeboshi, radish, cherry tomato

SERVING
TEMPERATURE:
hot or warm

MAIN DISH
PORK ONION RINGS

10oz (285g) pork butt (also called Boston butt or pork shoulder), cut into thin slices about 1½ in (4cm) wide and ⅛ in (0.3cm) thick (see note)

2 medium yellow onions, sliced into ½-in (1.25cm) rings (8–12 rings total)

½ cup potato starch or corn starch

1 tbsp vegetable oil

1 tbsp soy sauce

1 tbsp mirin

1 tbsp ketchup or steak sauce

1 tsp granulated sugar

Dash of salt

Sesame seeds (optional), to garnish

1. Wrap the pork slices around the onion rings. If the onion ring is too big, you can stack two rings together to make the inner ring smaller. Start wrapping from the wider end of the meat. Wrap it tightly, overlapping itself. (Think of wrapping tape on a tennis grip.) When adding on the next meat slice, make sure the two meat slices overlap. Coat each ring with a thin layer of starch.

2. In a large nonstick skillet, heat the oil over medium heat. Gently pat off any excess potato starch, and place 4 to 5 rings into the pan. Cook each side for 2 to 3 minutes. Transfer the cooked rings to a paper towel-lined plate to rest.

3. After all the rings are cooked, return the pan to the stovetop, and heat the soy sauce, mirin, ketchup, sugar, and salt over medium heat. When the sauce begins to boil, add the onion rings. Cook for 1 to 2 minutes, turning to coat in the sauce. Sprinkle with sesame seeds before serving.

STORAGE: Refrigerate up to 5 days; freeze up to 30 days.

NOTE: To more easily slice the meat, place it in the freezer for 90 minutes before slicing. Slice against the grain using a very sharp knife.

SIDE DISHES
BELL PEPPER FRITTATA

 4 SERVINGS 5 MIN 8 MIN

STORAGE: **Refrigerate up to 4 days.**

½ cup diced bell pepper (red or orange)

½ cup chopped broccoli

5 eggs

½ tsp salt

1 tbsp milk

1 tsp vegetable oil

1 tbsp grated cheese (any variety)

1 Place the bell pepper and broccoli in a small microwave-safe bowl, and microwave on high for 1 minute. In a second bowl, whisk the eggs with the salt and milk until combined.

2 In a small nonstick skillet or tamagoyaki pan, heat the oil over medium-low heat. Pour in half of the egg mixture. Sprinkle the bell pepper, broccoli, and cheese evenly over the top, and then pour in the remaining egg mixture. Cover with a lid, and cook for 4 to 5 minutes.

3 When the edges of the frittata are cooked and the center is still a bit runny, carefully cover the pan with a plate and flip it over, transferring the frittata to the plate. Place the frittata back in the pan and cook on the opposite side for 2 to 3 minutes or until puffy. Slice into squares.

SAUTÉED ZUCCHINI

 4 SERVINGS 5 MIN 8 MIN

STORAGE: **Refrigerate up to 3 days.**

2 tsp ghee or vegetable oil

1 medium zucchini, sliced

1 medium summer squash, sliced

Salt and freshly ground black pepper, to taste

Dried herb blend (optional), such as Italian or Provence

1 In a large nonstick skillet, heat the ghee over medium heat. Add the zucchini and summer squash. Cook each side for 3 to 4 minutes or until beginning to brown.

2 Season with salt and pepper, and sprinkle with dried herbs, if using. Stir gently to coat the vegetables with seasonings.

CHICKEN PATTIES
WITH OMELET FRIED RICE
AND BROCCOLI

The presentation and vivid colors of this bento make it popular with kids. Tofu lends moisture to the chicken patties, and the omelet covers a mound of savory fried rice.

NUTRITION PER BOX

500 calories
Total fat 28g
Cholesterol 219mg
Sodium 974mg
Total carb 40g
Protein 38g

COMPONENTS

MAIN DISH Chicken Patties (page 46)

SIDE DISHES Omelet Fried Rice (page 47)
Broccoli (page 39)

GARNISH cherry tomato

SERVING TEMPERATURE: warm or hot

MAIN DISH
CHICKEN PATTIES

 4 SERVINGS

 10 MIN

 10 MIN

STORAGE: Refrigerate up to 4 days, or freeze up to 15 days.

For the patties

10oz (395g) firm tofu

1lb (450g) ground chicken or turkey

¼ cup panko (Japanese bread crumbs)

1 tbsp milk

½ tsp salt

½ tsp freshly ground black pepper

2 tsp vegetable oil, divided

For the sauce

1½ tbsp soy sauce

1½ tbsp ketchup

1½ tsp granulated sugar

Sesame seeds (optional), to garnish

1   Wrap the tofu in a double layer of paper towels or clean cotton dish towels to remove excess water. Place a heavy plate on top of the tofu, and let sit for 5 minutes to drain.

2   To make the patties, in a medium bowl, combine the chicken, panko, milk, salt, and pepper. Using your hands, add the the tofu to the mixture, breaking it into small pieces. After 1 to 2 minutes, the mixture will become smooth and even. Use both hands to gather the mixture and toss it into the bowl several times until the mixture becomes sticky and the surface is smooth.

3   Divide the mixture into 16 equal portions. Shape each portion into a ball and toss it from hand to hand to remove the air inside.

4   In a large nonstick skillet, heat 1 teaspoon oil over medium heat. Cook the patties in batches, using a spatula to press them into the pan. Cook each side for 2 to 3 minutes. Add the remaining 1 teaspoon oil before cooking the second batch. Transfer the cooked patties to a plate.

5   To make the sauce, in a small bowl, whisk together all ingredients. After cooking the patties, return the skillet to low heat, and add the sauce. Place the patties in the pan and cook for 2 to 3 minutes or until the sauce has thickened. Gently flip the patties to coat them with the sauce. Sprinkle with sesame seeds, if using, before serving.

SIDE DISHES
OMELET FRIED RICE

 4 SERVINGS   5 MIN   15 MIN

STORAGE: **Refrigerate up to 3 days.**

2 tsp vegetable oil

¼ cup diced mushrooms

¼ cup diced onion

¼ cup diced carrot

¼ cup diced ham (optional)

¼ cup frozen shelled edamame or frozen mixed vegetables

2 tsp soy sauce

1 tbsp ketchup

½ tsp hot sauce (optional)

1½ cups cooked white rice

For the omelet

3 eggs

Pinch of salt

1 tsp vegetable oil

Ketchup (optional), to garnish

1 In a large skillet, heat the oil over medium heat. Add the mushrooms, onion, carrot, and ham, if using. Cook for 2 to 3 minutes or until they become aromatic. Stir in the edamame, soy sauce, ketchup, and hot sauce, if using. Cook for 1 to 2 minutes or until the vegetables are soft.

2 Reduce the heat to medium-low and add the rice. Gently stir, coating the rice with the sauce, and cook for 1 minute more. Divide the rice and vegetable mixture evenly among 4 bento boxes.

3 To make the omelet, in a medium bowl, whisk together the eggs and salt. In a small nonstick skillet, heat the oil over low heat, swirling to make sure the pan is fully coated.

4 Add a quarter of the egg mixture to the pan, and gently swirl so the egg covers the pan. Cook for 2 minutes or until the egg is just cooked. Starting at the edges, use a spatula to lift the egg from the pan, and then flip the pan to let the omelet fall on one serving of fried rice. Repeat this step to make three more omelets. Garnish the omelets with a squiggle of ketchup, if desired.

BROCCOLI

See recipe on **page 39;** do not include optional crab.

BACON TOFU ROLL

WITH SHISHITO PEPPERS, MISO EGGPLANT, AND KABOCHA

Bacon and miso give this bento wonderful depth of flavor. For a fully vegetarian bento, omit the bacon and panfry just the tofu.

COMPONENTS

MAIN DISH	Bacon Tofu Roll (page 50)
SIDE DISHES	Shishito Peppers (page 50)
	Miso Eggplant (page 51)
	Kabocha (page 51)
STAPLE	Jasmine Rice (page 153; 1/3 cup per serving)
GARNISH	umeboshi, lemon

SERVING TEMPERATURE: hot or warm

MAIN DISH
BACON TOFU ROLL

 2 SERVINGS

 5 MIN

 10 MIN

6oz (170g) firm or extra-firm tofu

3 slices bacon or prosciutto, cut in half

1 tsp soy sauce

1 tsp mirin

1 tsp water

1 Wrap the tofu in a clean cotton dish towel and place an empty bowl on the tofu for 3 minutes to press out excess water. Cut the tofu vertically into 6 slices.

2 Wrap 1 piece of bacon around each piece of tofu. Make sure the edges of the bacon overlap.

3 Heat a large nonstick skillet over medium heat. When hot, place the tofu rolls in the pan, seam side down. Over medium-low heat, cook each side for 3 to 4 minutes. Before flipping the tofu, make sure that the overlapping part of the bacon is set. Drain excess rendered fat from the pan.

4 Add the soy sauce, mirin, and water to the pan. Cook for 1 to 2 minutes, turning the bacon tofu rolls to coat with the sauce.

STORAGE: **Refrigerate up to 3 days.**

SIDE DISHES
SHISHITO PEPPERS

 2 SERVINGS 3 MIN 5 MIN

STORAGE: **Refrigerate up to 3 days.**

1 tsp vegetable oil

2 cups whole shishito peppers, washed and patted dry

Pinch of salt

1 lemon wedge

1 In a large nonstick skillet, heat the oil over medium to medium-high heat. Add the peppers and cook for 4 to 5 minutes. Turn the peppers occasionally to blister each side.

2 Sprinkle with salt and lemon juice just before serving so the peppers remain crunchy.

MISO EGGPLANT

 2 SERVINGS   5 MIN   10 MIN

STORAGE: **Refrigerate up to 3 days.**

½ tbsp miso

1 tbsp mayonnaise

¼ tsp sesame oil

¼ tsp granulated sugar

½ small eggplant, sliced ¼-½ in (1-1.5cm) thick

1 Preheat the oven to 355°F (180°C). Line a baking sheet with foil.

2 In a small bowl, whisk together the miso, mayonnaise, sesame oil, and sugar until smooth.

3 Score one side of the eggplant slices and spread a layer of miso paste on that side. Place on the prepared baking sheet, paste side up, and bake for 8 to 10 minutes.

KABOCHA

 2 SERVINGS   5 MIN   5 MIN

STORAGE: **Refrigerate up to 3 days; freeze up to 15 days.**

1 tsp vegetable oil or olive oil

6-8 slices kabocha (Japanese pumpkin), seeds removed, about ¼ in (.5cm) thick

Pinch of salt

Pinch of paprika or chili powder (optional)

1 In a large skillet, heat the oil over medium-low heat. When hot, cook the kabocha slices for 2 to 3 minutes on each side. Sprinkle with salt and paprika, if using, before serving.

GLAZED PORK BELLY
WITH SOY EGG AND
SPICY CUCUMBER

Tender pork belly in a delicious soy sauce glaze makes a hearty winter meal, especially when paired with a savory soy egg, jasmine rice, and crisp cucumber.

NUTRITION PER BOX

486 calories
Total fat 34g
Cholesterol 134mg
Sodium 1,662mg
Total carb 31g
Protein 13g

COMPONENTS

MAIN DISH	Glazed Pork Belly (page 54)
SIDE DISHES	Soy Eggs (page 55)
	Spicy Cucumber (page 55)
STAPLE	Jasmine Rice (page 153; ⅓ cup per serving)
GARNISH	umeboshi, cherry tomato

SERVING TEMPERATURE: warm

MAIN DISH
GLAZED PORK BELLY

4 SERVINGS 5 MIN 20 MIN

STORAGE: **Refrigerate up to 3 days; freeze up to 30 days.**

8oz (225g) pork belly, skin removed and cut into ½-in (1.25cm) slices

2 tbsp soy sauce

1 tbsp dark soy sauce (or regular soy sauce)

1 tbsp cooking sake

1 tbsp brown or granulated sugar

¾ cup water

1 spring onion or 2 scallions, cut into 1½-in (4cm) pieces

3–4 slices of fresh ginger

2–3 garlic cloves, chopped or sliced

1 Pat the pork belly dry with paper towels or a clean cotton dish towel. Heat a large nonstick skillet over medium to medium-high heat. Sear the pork belly for 3 minutes on each side or until golden brown.

2 Drain the rendered fat from the pan, and rinse the pork belly under hot running water to remove the grease on the surface.

3 Put the pork belly back into the pan, and add the remaining ingredients. Cover and cook over medium heat for 10 minutes. Remove the lid, and simmer for 2 to 3 minutes to thicken the sauce. Flip the pork occasionally to coat both sides with the sauce. Refrigerate with the sauce until ready to assemble your bento.

SIDE DISHES
SOY EGGS

 4 SERVINGS   3 MIN   10 MIN

STORAGE: Refrigerate up to 5 days with the marinade.

2 large eggs

For the marinade

¼ cup soy sauce

¼ cup mirin

¼ cup cooking sake

½ cup water

¼ tsp grated fresh ginger

¼ tsp minced garlic

1 To make the marinade, in a small saucepan, combine all ingredients and bring to a boil. Boil for 1 to 2 minutes, and then set aside to cool.

2 Bring a large pot of water to a boil. Gently add the eggs, making sure they are fully submerged. Boil for 6 to 7 minutes for runny yolks or 8 to 9 minutes for fully set yolks. Transfer the eggs to a bowl of ice water to cool.

3 Peel the eggs and place them in a lidded container. Add the marinade and turn to coat. Secure the lid and refrigerate for at least 1 to 2 days before eating.

SPICY
CUCUMBER

 4 SERVINGS   10 MIN   NONE

STORAGE: Refrigerate up to 4 days.

3 Persian cucumbers or 1½ English cucumbers, quartered and cut into 2-in (5cm) pieces

1 tsp salt

1 tbsp soy sauce

1½ tsp doubanjiang (chili bean paste)

2 tsp balsamic vinegar

2 tsp granulated sugar

1 tsp sesame oil

1 garlic clove, grated

1 spring onion or 2 scallions, finely chopped

1 tsp sesame seeds (optional)

1 In a medium bowl, use your hands to mix the cucumbers with the salt. Let sit for 5 minutes.

2 In a small bowl, whisk the remaining ingredients until the sugar is fully dissolved.

3 Rinse and drain the cucumbers and then add them to the soy sauce mixture. Let them sit for at least 5 minutes before serving, or refrigerate up to 4 days. Sprinkle with sesame seeds, if using, before serving.

SUSHI SANDWICHES

Sushi rice and nori are wrapped around a savory filling to create a tidy, portable package. This bento includes two popular fillings—ginger pork and ham with egg—but you can use other fillings as well.

COMPONENTS

FILLINGS   Ginger Pork (page 58)
Ham & Egg (page 58)

GARNISH   fresh mint

SERVING TEMPERATURE: warm or cold

FILLINGS
GINGER PORK

2 SERVINGS   5 MIN   5 MIN

STORAGE: **Refrigerate up to 5 days; freeze up to 30 days.**

1 tsp vegetable oil

½ cup julienned carrot

6oz (170g) ground pork or thinly sliced pork butt

2 tbsp grated fresh ginger

1 tbsp cooking sake

2 tbsp soy sauce

2 tbsp mirin

1 tsp granulated sugar (optional)

1 In a medium nonstick skillet, heat the oil over medium heat. Add the carrot and cook for 2 minutes or until soft. Add the pork and cook for 1 minute more.

2 Add the ginger, sake, soy sauce, mirin, and sugar, if using. Cook, stirring constantly, for 2 minutes or until the pork is fully cooked.

HAM & EGG

2 SERVINGS   2 MIN   10 MIN

STORAGE: **Refrigerate up to 3 days.**

2 eggs

Pinch of salt

1 tbsp milk

4oz (110g) thick-cut ham

1 tsp vegetable oil

1 In a small bowl, whisk the eggs with the salt and milk. Set aside.

2 Cut the ham into two squares, each about 3 x 3 inches (7.5 x 7.5cm). Heat a nonstick skillet over medium heat. Cook the ham on each side for 2 minutes until beginning to brown. Remove the ham and set aside.

3 In the same skillet, heat the oil over medium-low heat. Add the eggs and cook for 1 to 2 minutes or until the edges are set. Using a spatula, gently fold the egg over on itself to form a rectangle. Cook for 1 minute more, and then transfer to a cutting board to cool.

4 Cut the egg in half and fold if needed so the pieces are the same size as the ham slices. Stack the ham and egg.

SUSHI SANDWICH ASSEMBLY

STORAGE: **Refrigerate up to 5 days.**

4 sheets sushi seaweed (nori)

1½ cups cooked sushi rice, hot or warm

1 batch Ginger Pork Filling

1 batch Ham & Egg Filling

2–4 butter lettuce leaves

1 Spread a piece of plastic wrap on a work surface. The plastic wrap should be slightly larger than your seaweed sheets. Place 1 seaweed sheet on the plastic wrap, shiny side down.

2 Place ¼ cup of rice at the center of the seaweed, and spread the rice a little bit to create a square shape. Add a layer of filling. (For the ginger pork, place 1–2 lettuce leaves on the rice before adding the filling.) Cover the filling with 2 tablespoons of rice. It should look like bread on a sandwich.

3 Wrap the seaweed around the rice and filling. Fold it down from the top, up from the bottom, and then from the left and right sides. Wrap the sushi sandwich tightly with the plastic wrap and shape it into an even square. Repeat with the remaining ingredients to create a total of four sushi sandwiches, two of each filling.

4 Let the wrapped sandwiches sit for 2 to 3 minutes before cutting them in half. Rinse the knife before cutting to prevent the rice from sticking, and cut straight through the plastic wrap.

TERIYAKI CHICKEN
WITH EDAMAME EGG ROLL AND SAUTÉED SPINACH

Enjoy the sweet and savory flavor of teriyaki chicken accompanied by tender greens and a colorful egg roll. The teriyaki sauce is also delicious with salmon, tofu, or beef.

NUTRITION PER BOX

494 calories
Total fat 21g
Cholesterol 326mg
Sodium 1,178mg
Total carb 32g
Protein 43g

COMPONENTS

MAIN DISH	Teriyaki Chicken (page 62)
SIDE DISHES	Edamame Egg Roll (page 63) Sautéed Spinach (page 63)
STAPLE	Jasmine Rice (page 153; ⅓ cup per serving)
GARNISH	umeboshi, sesame seeds, cherry tomato

SERVING TEMPERATURE: hot or warm

MAIN DISH
TERIYAKI CHICKEN

 2 SERVINGS 5 MIN 10 MIN

STORAGE: **Refrigerate up to 5 days; freeze up to 15 days.**

3 boneless, skinless
  chicken thighs

1 tbsp soy sauce

1 tbsp mirin

1 tbsp cooking sake

1-2 tsp granulated sugar

1 Cut each chicken thigh into 3 to 4 pieces. Heat a large nonstick skillet over medium heat. When hot, place the chicken in the pan and cook for 2 to 3 minutes until golden brown. Turn the chicken pieces and cook on the opposite side for 2 to 3 minutes until golden.

2 Add the soy sauce, mirin, sake, and sugar. Stir to coat the chicken thighs with the sauce. Cook for 3 to 4 minutes to thicken the sauce.

SIDE DISHES
EDAMAME EGG ROLL

 2 SERVINGS   5 MIN   10 MIN

STORAGE: **Refrigerate up to 4 days.**

2 large eggs

2 tsp water

Pinch of salt

Pinch of bonito stock powder, such as Hondashi, or 1 tsp soy sauce

2 tbsp shelled edamame

2 tbsp diced carrots

1 tsp vegetable oil

1 In a small bowl, whisk the eggs, water, salt, and bonito stock powder. In a second small microwave-safe bowl, microwave the edamame and carrots for 1 to 2 minutes or until tender.

2 In a tamagoyaki pan or nonstick skillet, heat the oil over medium-low heat. (If you're not using a nonstick pan, use an additional ½ teaspoon oil.) When hot, pour in one third of the egg mixture. After 30 seconds or when the egg is partially cooked, sprinkle the edamame and carrots evenly over the egg.

3 Using a spatula, gently roll up the egg, starting at the edge opposite the handle and rolling toward the handle. Push the rolled egg to the side of the pan opposite the handle.

4 Pour the remaining egg mixture into the pan. Using a spatula, lift the rolled egg so it can be coated with a new layer of egg mixture. Repeat step 3, rolling the egg toward the handle. Remove from the heat and let the completed egg roll rest for 3 minutes in the pan before slicing.

SAUTÉED SPINACH

 2 SERVINGS   5 MIN   🔥 5 MIN

STORAGE: **Refrigerate up to 3 days.**

1 tbsp vegetable oil or olive oil

Pinch of garlic powder or 1 garlic clove, minced

1 carrot, thinly sliced

1 bunch of spinach, about 8oz (225g), roughly chopped

Pinch of salt

1 In a large nonstick skillet, heat the oil over medium to medium-high heat. When hot, add the garlic and carrot. Sauté the carrot for 2 to 3 minutes. Add the spinach and salt, and sauté for 1 to 2 minutes or until tender.

PAN-
ASIAN
BENTO

MAPO TOFU WITH PICKLED CUCUMBER, EGG ROLL, AND SWEET JAPANESE PUMPKIN

Spicy and aromatic, this mapo tofu is a healthier version of the popular Chinese takeout dish. Sweet and tangy side dishes balance the spiciness of the tofu.

NUTRITION PER BOX

383 calories
Total fat 15g
Cholesterol 179mg
Sodium 944mg
Total carb 30g
Protein 29g

COMPONENTS

MAIN DISH	Mapo Tofu (page 68)
SIDE DISHES	Pickled Cucumber (page 69) Egg Roll (page 69) Sweet Japanese Pumpkin (page 31)
STAPLE	Jasmine Rice (page 153; ⅓ cup per serving)
GARNISH	cherry tomato

SERVING TEMPERATURE: hot or warm

MAIN DISH
MAPO TOFU

 4 SERVINGS 5 MIN 20 MIN

STORAGE: Refrigerate up to 3 days.

1½ tsp vegetable oil

½ tsp freshly ground Szechuan pepper (optional)

1 garlic clove, minced (optional)

½ lb ground turkey (you can substitute any other ground meat or plant-based meat substitute)

1 tbsp spicy bean sauce

1 tbsp spicy chili sauce, such as Laoganma

1 tsp soy sauce

8oz (22g) silken or firm tofu, cut into cubes

2 tbsp water

¼ tsp granulated sugar

½ tsp potato starch (optional)

1 In a large nonstick skillet, heat the oil over medium-low heat. Add the pepper and garlic, if using, and cook for 2 minutes or until fragrant. Add the turkey and cook for 2 minutes or until it is no longer pink.

2 Add the spicy bean sauce, spicy chili sauce, and soy sauce, and stir to combine. When the sauce begins to boil, push the turkey to the side of the pan, and add the tofu to the center of the pan. Add the water and cover. Cook for 3 minutes.

3 Remove the lid, gently push the turkey from the side of the pan, and mix it with the tofu. Sprinkle in the sugar, and reduce the heat to low.

4 If you desire a thicker sauce, in a small bowl, mix the potato starch with 1 teaspoon water. Pour the mixture into the pan, and gently stir to coat the tofu and turkey with the thickened sauce. Remove from the heat after 1 minute.

SIDE DISHES
PICKLED CUCUMBER

 4 SERVINGS 20 MIN NONE

STORAGE: **Refrigerate up to 7 days.**

1 cup thinly sliced
cucumber

1 tsp salt

2 tbsp rice vinegar

2 tsp granulated sugar

1 fresh chile, chopped
(optional)

1 Place the cucumbers in a small bowl. Sprinkle with salt and massage the cucumber until it is fully coated in salt. Let sit for 10 minutes.

2 Drain the liquid, and rinse the cucumber with running water. Add the rice vinegar and sugar. If you like spice, add the chile. Cover and refrigerate for at least 10 minutes before serving.

EGG ROLL

 4 SERVINGS 5 MIN 15 MIN

STORAGE: **Refrigerate up to 2 days.**

3 large eggs

1 tbsp mirin

Pinch of salt

½ tsp granulated sugar

Pinch of bonito stock
powder, such as
Hondashi (optional)

1 tsp vegetable oil

1 In a medium bowl, whisk together the eggs, mirin, salt, sugar, and bonito powder, if using, until well combined. In a tamagoyaki pan or nonstick skillet, heat the oil over low heat. (If you're not using a nonstick pan, use an additional ½ teaspoon oil.)

2 Add half of the egg mixture to the pan and let cook, without stirring, until the bottom of the egg is set but the top is still a bit runny. Using a spatula, gently roll up the egg, starting at the edge opposite the handle and rolling toward the handle. Push the rolled egg to the side of the pan opposite the handle.

3 Pour the remaining egg mixture into the pan. Using a spatula, lift the rolled egg so it can be coated with a new layer of egg mixture. Repeat step 2, rolling the egg toward the handle. Remove from the heat and let the completed egg roll rest for 1 minute in the pan before slicing.

SWEET JAPANESE PUMPKIN

See recipe on **page 31**.

ROSE GYOZA
WITH SESAME VEGETABLES

Have your lunch break in this secret garden with blooming rose gyoza and aromatic blanched vegetables. This is the best method for cooking perfectly crispy gyoza and can be used for frozen premade gyoza as well.

COMPONENTS

MAIN DISH	Rose Gyoza (page 72)
SIDE DISH	Sesame Vegetables (page 73)
GARNISH	radish

SERVING TEMPERATURE: hot or warm

MAIN DISH
ROSE GYOZA

 4 SERVINGS   40 MIN   15 MIN

STORAGE: **Refrigerate up to 5 days;
freeze up to 30 days.**

48 gyoza or dumpling
wrappers

1 tsp vegetable oil

1 tbsp sesame oil

For the filling

1 lb (450g) ground pork or
turkey

4 tsp soy sauce

2 tsp sesame oil

½ tsp fish sauce
(optional)

½ tsp granulated sugar

3 garlic cloves, minced or
a pinch of garlic powder

1½ tsp minced fresh
ginger or ¼ tsp ground
ginger

1 scallion, finely chopped

1 To make the filling, in a large bowl, combine all the ingredients. Add up to ⅔ cup water, 1 tablespoon at a time, until the mixture is no longer able to absorb any more water. Cover and refrigerate for 15 minutes.

2 Line up 3 wrappers in a row with the edges slightly overlapped. Attach the overlapping parts by dabbing some water with your finger. Place 1 teaspoon of the filing at the center of each wrapper. Lightly dab water on the edges of all wrappers. Fold all wrappers in half widthwise, and seal the edges with water. Dab a little water on the wrappers, especially on the two ends, to prevent the gyoza rose from falling apart. Gently roll from left to right, and adjust the petals. Repeat to create 16 gyoza roses in total.

3 In a large nonstick skillet with a lid, heat the vegetable oil over medium heat. Place the gyoza in the pan with some space in between. (You may need to work in batches.) Add enough water to cover about one third of the gyoza, and then add the sesame oil. Cover and cook over medium-high heat for 5 to 6 minutes. Remove the lid, and reduce the heat to medium. Cook for 6 to 7 minutes or until the water has evaporated.

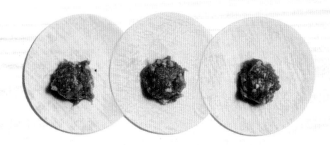

Arrange wrappers with edges overlapping. Place 1 teaspoon of filling in center of each wrapper.

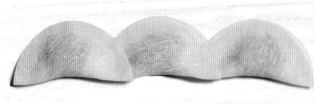

Moisten edges and fold up wrappers.

SIDE DISH
SESAME VEGETABLES

 4 SERVINGS   5 MIN   10 MIN

STORAGE: **Refrigerate up to 4 days; freeze up to 30 days.**

1½ cups chicken stock

1 tsp salt

2 cups broccoli florets, broken into bite-sized pieces

1 cup sliced carrots

1 cup sliced cucumber

2 tsp sesame oil

2 tsp soy sauce

2 tsp balsamic vinegar or red wine vinegar

1–1½ tsp chili oil or hot sauce

1 scallion, chopped (optional)

1 To a large saucepan or pot, add the chicken stock, salt, and 2 to 3 cups water. The liquid should be 4 to 5 inches (10–12cm) deep. Bring to a boil over high heat. Working in batches, add the broccoli and carrots to the boiling liquid. When the liquid begins to boil again after adding the vegetables, remove them with a slotted spoon and transfer to a large bowl.

2 Add the cucumbers to the bowl, and toss the vegetables with the sesame oil, soy sauce, vinegar, and chili oil. Sprinkle with scallions, if using.

Begin rolling from left to right.

GROUND TURKEY & CAPERS WITH CHAYOTE & MUSHROOM STIR-FRY, SCALLION EGG ROLL, AND PICKLED ONION

NUTRITION PER BOX

351 calories
Total fat 14g
Cholesterol 178mg
Sodium 817mg
Total carb 36g
Protein 21g

This Taiwanese-inspired bento includes chayote, a member of the gourd family that can be found in the produce section. Its smooth, light green skin is edible, and its flavor and texture are similar to summer squash.

COMPONENTS

MAIN DISH	Ground Turkey & Capers (page 76)
SIDE DISHES	Chayote & Mushroom Stir-Fry (page 77)
	Scallion Egg Roll (page 77)
	Pickled Onion (page 39)
STAPLE	Quinoa Rice (page 154; ⅓ cup per serving)
GARNISH	cherry tomato

SERVING TEMPERATURE:
hot or warm

MAIN DISH
GROUND TURKEY & CAPERS

 4 SERVINGS

 5 MIN

 10 MIN

STORAGE: Refrigerate up to 5 days; freeze up to 30 days.

1 tbsp vegetable oil

1 garlic clove, minced, or a pinch of garlic powder

2 fresh chiles, sliced (optional)

½ lb (225g) ground turkey (or any other ground meat or plant-based ground meat substitute)

1 tsp soy sauce

1 tsp cooking sake

3 tbsp capers, plus 1 tsp liquid from jar

½ tsp granulated sugar

1 cup diced green beans

Pinch of salt, to taste

1 In a large nonstick skillet, heat the oil over medium heat. Add the garlic and chiles, if using, and cook for 1 minute. Add the ground meat, soy sauce, and sake, and cook for 3 to 4 minutes until the meat is no longer pink.

2 Add the capers and liquid, sugar, and beans. Cook for 3 to 4 minutes. Stir occasionally to keep the capers mixed well with the beans and meat. Taste and season with salt, if needed.

SIDE DISHES

PICKLED ONION

See recipe on **page 39.**

CHAYOTE & MUSHROOM STIR-FRY

 4 SERVINGS   10 MIN   5 MIN

STORAGE: **Refrigerate up to 5 days.**

1 tsp vegetable oil
1½ cups sliced shitake mushrooms
Pinch of salt
3 chayote, thinly sliced or julienned
1 tbsp oyster sauce or thick soy sauce (soy paste)
1 tsp soy sauce
Pinch of freshly ground black pepper
Sesame oil (optional)

1 In a large nonstick skillet, heat the vegetable oil over medium heat. Add the mushrooms, and cook for 1 to 2 minutes or until soft. Increase the heat to medium-high, and add the salt and chayote. Cook for 3 to 4 minutes or until the chayote has softened.

2 Add the oyster sauce and soy sauce. Cook, stirring, for 1 to 2 minutes until the chayote is fully cooked. Sprinkle with pepper and a few drops of sesame oil, if using.

SCALLION EGG ROLL

 4 SERVINGS   3 MIN   15 MIN

STORAGE: **Refrigerate up to 3 days.**

3 large eggs
2 tbsp diced scallion
1 tsp furikake (Japanese rice seasoning) or ½ tsp toasted sesame seeds
Pinch of salt
¼ tsp soy sauce
1 tsp water
1 tsp vegetable oil

1 In a medium bowl, whisk together the eggs, scallion, furikake, salt, soy sauce, and water until well combined. In a tamagoyaki pan or nonstick skillet, heat the oil over low heat. (If you're not using a nonstick pan, use an additional ½ teaspoon oil.)

2 Add half of the egg mixture to the pan and let cook, without stirring, until the bottom of the egg is set but the top is still a bit runny.

3 Using a spatula, gently roll up the egg, starting at the edge opposite the handle and rolling toward the handle. Push the rolled egg to the side of the pan opposite the handle.

4 Pour the remaining egg mixture into the pan. Using a spatula, lift the rolled egg so it can be coated with a new layer of egg mixture. Repeat step 3, rolling the egg toward the handle. Remove from the heat and let the completed egg roll rest for 1 minute in the pan before slicing.

DAIKON STEWED PORK
WITH ASPARAGUS & SHRIMP AND
BEECH MUSHROOM STIR-FRY

A popular Taiwanese dish, lu rou fan, is the inspiration for this colorful bento. Daikon radish flavors the tender pork stew, which is accompanied by flavorful shrimp and asparagus and delicate beech mushrooms.

NUTRITION PER BOX

498 calories
Total fat 33g
Cholesterol 63mg
Sodium 645mg
Total carb 38g
Protein 15g

COMPONENTS

MAIN DISH	Daikon Stewed Pork (page 80)
SIDE DISHES	Asparagus & Shrimp (page 81) Beech Mushroom Stir-Fry (page 81)
STAPLE	Quinoa Rice (page 154; 1/3 cup per serving)
GARNISH	radish

SERVING TEMPERATURE:
hot or warm

MAIN DISH
DAIKON STEWED PORK

 8 SERVINGS 10 MIN 40 MIN

STORAGE: **Refrigerate up to 5 days; freeze up to 30 days.**

1 tsp vegetable oil

1lb (450g) pork belly, cut into bite-sized pieces

3 shallots, sliced,

3 garlic cloves, minced, or ½ tsp garlic powder

2 scallions, finely sliced (optional)

1 tbsp brown sugar

1 tbsp oyster sauce or thick soy sauce

1 tbsp soy sauce

1 tsp freshly ground black pepper

3 cups daikon radish wedges

1 tbsp cooking sake

Salt, to taste

1 Set a multicooker, such as an Instant Pot, to Saute. Add the oil. When hot, add the pork belly and cook for 4 to 5 minutes or until the meat is no longer pink.

2 Add the shallots, garlic, and scallions, and cook for 2 minutes or until fragrant. Add the brown sugar, oyster sauce, soy sauce, and black pepper. Cook for 1 to 2 minutes more, stirring occasionally.

3 Turn off Saute. Add the radish and sake, and pour in water until the water covers about two thirds of the pork and radish mixture. Secure the lid, and set to Pressure (High) for 25 minutes. Allow the pressure to release naturally for 10 minutes. Quick release the remaining pressure. Taste, and season with salt as needed.

SIDE DISHES
ASPARAGUS & SHRIMP

 4 SERVINGS   10 MIN   10 MIN

STORAGE: **Refrigerate up to 3 days.**

12 medium raw shrimp, peeled and deveined

1 tbsp cooking sake

Pinch of salt

1 tsp olive oil or vegetable oil

1 garlic clove, minced, or a pinch of garlic powder

Pinch of red pepper flakes (optional)

1 lb (450g) asparagus, trimmed and cut into bite-size pieces

1 tsp soy sauce

Freshly ground black pepper, to taste

1 tsp lemon juice

1 Place the shrimp in a medium bowl and toss with the sake and a pinch of salt. Marinate for 5 minutes. Pat the shrimp dry with paper towels. Set aside.

2 In a large skillet, heat the oil, garlic, and red pepper flakes, if using, over medium heat. Add the asparagus and cook for 2 minutes.

3 Add the shrimp and soy sauce, and cook for 2 minutes or until the shrimp become pink and opaque. Remove from the heat. Sprinkle with salt, pepper, and lemon juice.

BEECH MUSHROOM STIR-FRY

 4 SERVINGS   5 MIN   10 MIN

STORAGE: **Refrigerate up to 3 days.**

1 tsp vegetable oil or olive oil

1 cup beech mushrooms, broken into pieces, or sliced mushrooms

1 yellow bell pepper, sliced

1 red bell pepper, sliced

1 tsp soy sauce

1 tbsp oyster sauce or thick soy sauce

¼ tsp sesame oil

1 In a large nonstick skillet, heat the oil over medium heat. Add the beech mushrooms and sauté for 1 to 2 minutes or until soft.

2 Add the bell peppers, soy sauce, oyster sauce, and sesame oil. Stir occasionally and cook for 3 to 4 minutes.

MANDARIN CHICKEN
WITH SAUTÉED CHARD & MUSHROOM AND TOMATO SALAD

Inspired by one of the most popular products in the Trader Joe's freezer, this bento features a healthier version of tangy Mandarin orange chicken paired with garlicky sautéed chard and savory tomato salad.

NUTRITION PER BOX

267 calories
Total fat 7g
Cholesterol 70mg
Sodium 671mg
Total carb 32g
Protein 20g

COMPONENTS

MAIN DISH   Mandarin Chicken (page 84)

SIDE DISHES   Sautéed Chard & Mushrooms (page 85)
Tomato Salad (page 85)

STAPLE   Jasmine Rice (page 153; ⅓ cup per serving)

SERVING TEMPERATURE: hot or warm

MAIN DISH
MANDARIN CHICKEN

4 SERVINGS 25 MIN 15 MIN

STORAGE: **Refrigerate up to 4 days; freeze up to 15 days.**

2 boneless, skinless
  chicken thighs

1 tsp vegetable oil

2 tsp granulated sugar

Juice and pulp of 1 orange

1 tsp balsamic vinegar

1 tsp honey (optional)

For the marinade

1 tsp soy sauce

1 tsp balsamic vinegar

1 tsp orange marmalade

Pinch of salt and freshly
  ground black pepper

1. In a medium bowl, whisk together all marinade ingredients. Add the chicken to the marinade, turning to coat. Cover and refrigerate for at least 20 minutes or overnight.

2. In a large nonstick skillet, heat the oil over medium-high heat. Add the chicken, and cook for 3 to 5 minutes until the chicken is cooked and has a golden, crispy surface.

3. In a small saucepan, heat the sugar over low heat until it melts and turns brown. Add the orange juice, orange pulp, and balsamic vinegar. Increase the heat to high, and bring to a boil.

4. When the sauce begins to boil, remove the pan from the heat and add the chicken, turning to coat. Add the honey to increase the sauce, if desired.

SIDE DISHES

SAUTÉED CHARD & MUSHROOMS

 4 SERVINGS 5 MIN 10 MIN

STORAGE: **Refrigerate up to 3 days.**

2 tsp vegetable oil or olive oil

1 garlic clove, chopped, or a pinch of garlic powder

Pinch of red pepper flakes (optional)

Pinch of za'atar or sumac (optional)

$2/3$ cup sliced mushrooms (4-5 mushrooms)

1 lb (450g) Swiss chard, chopped, stems and leaves kept separate

½ tsp soy sauce

Pinch of salt

1 In a large nonstick skillet, heat the oil over medium heat. Add the garlic, red pepper flakes, and za'atar, if using, and cook for 30 seconds or until fragrant. Add the mushrooms and chard stems, and cook for 2 minutes.

2 Add the chard leaves, and cook for 1 minute. Add the soy sauce and salt. Cook for 1 minute more or until the chard leaves are soft.

TOMATO SALAD

 4 SERVINGS 5 MIN 3 MIN

STORAGE: **Refrigerate up to 2 days.**

2 tsp oyster sauce or thick soy sauce (soy paste)

½ tsp grated fresh ginger

½ tsp granulated sugar

2 large beefsteak tomatoes, sliced into wedges ½-in (1cm) thick

1 In a medium bowl, whisk the oyster sauce, ginger, and sugar until well combined. Add the tomato wedges, and toss gently to cover the tomatoes with the dressing.

PINEAPPLE SHRIMP
WITH SUGAR SNAP PEAS AND HONEY LEMON RADISH

As if you're enjoying a warm breeze from the ocean, this bento combines sweet tropical fruit and succulent shrimp in a refreshing dish. It's paired with crunchy sugar snap peas and sweet and spicy radish.

COMPONENTS

MAIN DISH   Pineapple Shrimp (page 88)

SIDE DISHES   Sugar Snap Peas (page 89)
Honey Lemon Radishes (page 89)

STAPLE   Jasmine Rice (page 153; 1/3 cup per serving)

SERVING TEMPERATURE: hot or warm

MAIN DISH
PINEAPPLE SHRIMP

 4 SERVINGS   15 MIN   10 MIN

STORAGE: **Refrigerate up to 4 days.**

16 large raw shrimp,
  peeled and deveined,
  tail on

1 tbsp cooking sake

¼ tsp salt

2 tbsp potato starch or
  corn starch

3 tbsp vegetable oil

1 cup diced pineapple
  (fresh or canned)

2 tbsp mayonnaise

1 tbsp plain yogurt

1 tbsp freshly squeezed
  lemon juice or lime juice

1 tsp granulated sugar

1 Rinse the shrimp, and use a knife to cut along the vein of the shrimp to create a slit about ¼ inch (6mm) deep. (This deep cut will cause the shrimp to curl into tight balls when cooked.) Place the shrimp in a small bowl, and add the sake and salt. Let sit for 5 minutes.

2 Pat the shrimp dry, and coat with potato starch. Let the shrimp rest for 3 minutes until the potato starch coating becomes moist.

3 In a large nonstick skillet, heat the oil over medium heat. Sear the shrimp for 2 to 3 minutes on each side until the shrimp are opaque and the surface is crunchy. Transfer to a paper towel–lined plate and set aside.

4 If using fresh pineapple, in the same pan, sauté the pineapple chunks for 2 to 3 minutes or until soft. (If using canned pineapple, skip this step.) Turn off the heat.

5 In a small bowl, whisk together the mayonnaise, yogurt, lemon juice, and sugar. Add the mixture, pineapple, and shrimp to the pan with the pineapple. Gently stir to combine. Taste and add more sugar if the pineapple is too sour.

SIDE DISHES
SUGAR SNAP PEAS

 4 SERVINGS   5 MIN   10 MIN

STORAGE: **Refrigerate up to 4 days.**

3 cups sugar snap peas, trimmed

1 tbsp olive oil

2 garlic cloves, sliced, or ¼ tsp garlic powder

1 cup julienned carrot

⅔ cup thinly sliced king oyster mushrooms, or cremini mushrooms

1 tsp oyster sauce or thick soy sauce (soy paste)

Pinch of salt

1 Bring a pot of water to a boil. Blanch the peas for 30 seconds and then drain. (Alternatively, place the peas in a medium bowl. Spray some water on the peas, cover, and microwave for 1 to 2 minutes until the peas are bright green.)

2 In a large nonstick skillet, heat the oil over medium heat. Add the garlic and cook for 1 minute. Add the carrot and cook for 1 to 2 minutes more. Increase the heat to high, and add the mushrooms. Sauté for 1 to 2 minutes. Add the peas, oyster sauce, and salt. Cook for 30 seconds, stirring frequently, to coat the vegetables with the sauce.

HONEY LEMON
RADISHES

 4 SERVINGS    35 MIN   NONE

STORAGE: **Refrigerate up to 15 days.**

8–10 red radishes, whole or cut into quarters

1 tsp salt

3 tbsp freshly squeezed lemon juice

2 tbsp honey

1 In a medium bowl, toss the radishes with the salt. Let sit for 30 minutes.

2 Rinse the radishes, and pat dry. In a small bowl, toss the radishes with the lemon juice and honey. To decorate the radishes with spots, use the end of a plastic straw to carve out small circles from the radish skin.

SAVORY POACHED CHICKEN WITH ZOODLES

This bento is a low-carb version of the popular Taiwanese night market snack. With zoodles taking the place of rice, it contains delicately poached chicken, vibrant vegetables, and simple seasonings. Don't forget to shake it well before eating!

NUTRITION PER BOX

311 calories
Total fat 23g
Cholesterol 105mg
Sodium 243mg
Total carb 7g
Protein 21g

COMPONENTS

MAIN DISH   Savory Poached Chicken (page 92)

SIDE DISH   Zoodles (page 92)

GARNISH   radish

SERVING TEMPERATURE: warm or cold

MAIN DISH & SIDE DISH
SAVORY POACHED CHICKEN
WITH ZOODLES

 4 SERVINGS 10 MIN 35 MIN

STORAGE: **Refrigerate up to 5 days.**

1lb (450g) bone-in chicken leg quarters

2 tsp salt

2 star anise pods

4 tbsp whole Szechuan peppercorns, or 1½ tsp ground Szechuan pepper

1 tsp freshly ground black pepper

5–6 slices fresh ginger

2 scallions, cut into 2-in (5cm) pieces

2 cups broccoli florets

2 cups cauliflower florets

1 cup sliced carrots

8 cups zucchini noodles

4 tsp sesame oil

Salt, to taste

1 Place the chicken in a large pot and add cold water until the chicken is fully covered. Add the salt, star anise, peppercorns, black pepper, ginger, and scallions. Bring to a boil over high heat. Cook for 5 minutes, skimming off any foam that forms on the surface. Remove from the heat, cover, and let sit for 10 minutes.

2 Fill a large bowl with 3 cups ice water. Using tongs, transfer the chicken to the ice water bath. (Do not discard the broth in the pot.)

3 When cool to the touch, remove the chicken from the ice water, and place on a cutting board. (Do not discard the ice bath.) Set aside.

4   Strain any solids from the broth, and discard. Bring the broth to a boil, and add the broccoli, cauliflower, and carrots. When the liquid begins to boil again, use a slotted spoon to transfer the vegetables to the same ice bath used for the chicken. Remove when fully cooled.

5   Bring the broth back to a boil, and blanch the zucchini noodles for 30 seconds. Reserve the remaining broth.

6   Divide the zucchini noodles and vegetables evenly among four bento boxes. Using a knife or poultry shears, cut the chicken into bite-sized pieces and discard the bones.

7   Add the chicken to the bento boxes and drizzle each serving with 1 teaspoon sesame oil, 2 tablespoons reserved broth, and a sprinkle of salt. Cover and shake well before eating.

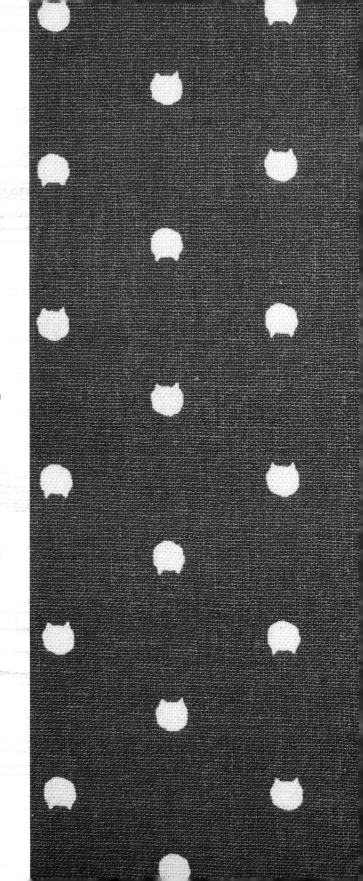

BIBIMBAP BENTO

Enjoy a healthy and delightful lunch with a traditional Korean dish. Each of the simple side dishes contributes a distinct flavor to the whole bento. Mix everything together or eat each side dish separately.

422 calories
Total fat 24g
Cholesterol 225mg
Sodium 980mg
Total carb 30g
Protein 22g

COMPONENTS

MAIN DISH   Spicy Beef (page 96)

SIDE DISHES   Sesame Spinach (page 96)
Ginger Carrot (page 97)
Sweet Pickled Radish (page 97)
Sunny Egg (page 97)
Pickled Cucumber (page 69)

STAPLE   Jasmine Rice (page 153; ⅓ cup per serving)

SERVING TEMPERATURE:
warm or hot

MAIN DISH
SPICY BEEF

 2 SERVINGS 15 MIN 5 MIN

STORAGE: **Refrigerate up to 5 days; freeze up to 15 days.**

3–4oz (85–115g) thinly sliced skirt steak or flank steak (lean ground beef or thinly sliced pork or lamb can also be used)

1 tsp vegetable oil

Dash of hot sauce (optional)

Pinch of sesame seeds (optional)

For the marinade

1 tbsp gochujang (Korean chili paste)

1 tsp sesame oil

1 tsp soy sauce

1 tsp mirin

1 tsp cooking sake

1½ tsp pear or apple purée or finely grated pear or apple

1 In a medium bowl, whisk together all marinade ingredients. Add the meat and set aside to marinate for 10 minutes.

2 In a large nonstick skillet, heat the oil over medium heat. Add the meat along with the marinade. Cook for 3 to 4 minutes or until the meat is fully cooked. Add hot sauce and sprinkle with sesame seeds before serving, if desired.

SIDE DISHES
SESAME SPINACH

 2 SERVINGS 5 MIN 1 MIN

STORAGE: **Refrigerate up to 3 days.**

1 bunch of spinach, about 8oz (225g), roughly chopped

1 tsp sesame oil

Pinch of salt

Pinch of roasted sesame seeds

Pinch of garlic powder (optional)

1 Bring a pot of water to a boil, and blanch the spinach for 20 seconds. Remove the spinach, and drain.

2 In a medium bowl, toss the spinach with the sesame oil, salt, sesame seeds, and garlic powder, if desired.

PICKLED CUCUMBER

See recipe on **page 69.**

GINGER CARROT

 2 SERVINGS 5 MIN 1 MIN

STORAGE: **Refrigerate up to 3 days.**

1 carrot, julienned

½ tsp grated fresh ginger, or a pinch of ground ginger

1 tsp sesame oil

Pinch of salt

Pinch of toasted sesame seeds

1 Bring a pot of water to a boil, and blanch the carrot for 40 seconds. Remove the carrot, and drain.

2 In a medium bowl, toss the carrot with the ginger, sesame oil, salt, and sesame seeds.

SWEET PICKLED RADISH

 2 SERVINGS 15 MIN NONE

STORAGE: **Refrigerate up to 5 days.**

½ cup julienned daikon radish

1 tsp salt

1 tbsp granulated sugar

1 tbsp rice vinegar

1 To a medium bowl, add the radish and salt. Massage the radish, and let it sit for 5 minutes.

2 Rinse the radish with water, and then squeeze to drain. Mix the radish with the sugar and rice vinegar, and let it sit for 5 to 10 minutes.

SUNNY EGG

 2 SERVINGS NONE 5 MIN

STORAGE: **Refrigerate up to 3 days.**

2 tsp vegetable oil or olive oil

2 eggs

1 In a medium nonstick skillet, heat the oil over medium heat. When hot, crack the eggs into the skillet carefuly with yolks intact. Cook for 1 minute or until the edges of the eggs begin to brown.

2 Reduce the heat to low, and cover. Cook for 2 to 3 minutes or until the whites are set but the yolks are runny. Take care not to break the yolk when assembling the bento.

JIAO MA CHICKEN
WITH CABBAGE & CUCUMBER
SALAD AND COCONUT RICE

Inspired by the flavors of jiao ma chicken, a favorite Taiwanese dish, and nasi lemak, a renowned Malay dish, this bento features tender spiced chicken paired with refreshing cabbage salad and fragrant coconut rice.

COMPONENTS

MAIN DISH Jiao Ma Chicken (page 100)

SIDE DISHES Coconut Rice (page 100)
Cabbage & Cucumber Salad (page 101)

GARNISH cherry tomato

SERVING TEMPERATURE:
warm or cold

MAIN DISH
JIAO MA CHICKEN

 4 SERVINGS

 25 MIN

 10 MIN

2 boneless, skinless chicken breasts, sliced in half lengthwise to ¾-in (2cm) thick

1 tsp soy sauce

1 tsp vegetable oil

1 Place the chicken in a lidded container or resealable bag, and add the soy sauce. Turn to coat. Marinate for 15 minutes or more.

2 In a large nonstick skillet, heat the oil over medium to medium-high heat. Add the chicken and cook for 2 to 3 minutes on each side. Let sit for 2 minutes before slicing.

STORAGE: **Refrigerate up to 3 days; freeze up to 15 days.**

SIDE DISHES
COCONUT RICE

 4 SERVINGS 25 MIN 25 MIN

STORAGE: **Refrigerate up to 4 days; freeze up to 10 days.**

¾ cup short-grain white rice

¼ cup black rice

1 cup water

1 cup light unsweetened coconut milk

2 stalks lemongrass, trimmed and finely chopped

4–5 slices fresh ginger

3–4 garlic cloves, halved

Coconut flakes (optional), to garnish

1 Rinse the white and black rice, and then soak the rice in water for 20 to 25 minutes. Drain.

2 In a small saucepan, combine the rice, water, coconut milk, lemongrass, ginger, and garlic. Bring to a boil. When boiling, stir quickly to make sure no rice is stuck to the bottom of the saucepan. Cover and cook for 10 minutes over low heat. (Do not remove the lid.)

3 Remove from the heat and let sit, covered, for 15 minutes. Remove the lid, and remove the lemongrass, ginger, and garlic. (These can be discarded.) Fluff with a fork. Garnish with coconut flakes, if using, before serving.

CABBAGE & CUCUMBER SALAD

 4 SERVINGS 5 MIN NONE

STORAGE: **Refrigerate up to 2 days.**

1 cucumber, julienned

2 cups thinly sliced
cabbage

1 tbsp vegetable oil

For the sauce

½ bunch cilantro,
chopped

2-3 garlic cloves, minced

1-2 frsh red chiles
(optional), finely
chopped

2 tbsp chopped peanuts
(optional)

½ tsp freshly ground
Szechuan pepper
(optional)

1 tsp sesame seeds

1 tbsp fish sauce

1 tbsp black vinegar or
balsamic vinegar

1 tbsp soy sauce

Juice of 1 lime

2 tbsp granulated sugar

1 tbsp sesame oil

1. In a large bowl, whisk together all the sauce ingredients. Reserve one third of the sauce in a separate container. Add the cucumber and cabbage to the sauce and massage to coat.

2. Before serving, pour the reserved sauce over the chicken.

TANDOORI CHICKEN SANDWICH WITH
TOMATO & AVOCADO SALAD

A light lunch with the right amount of spice and freshness for summer days, this chicken sandwich is convenient to carry and easy to eat wherever you are. Paired with sweet and sour tomato and avocado salad, it makes a fulfilling and nutritious lunch.

NUTRITION PER BOX

492 calories
Total fat 23g
Cholesterol 149mg
Sodium 1,145mg
Total carb 78g
Protein 47g

COMPONENTS

MAIN DISH   Tandoori Chicken Sandwich (page 104)

SIDE DISH   Tomato & Avocado Salad (page 105)

SERVING TEMPERATURE: warm or cold

MAIN DISH
TANDOORI CHICKEN SANDWICH

 4 SERVINGS   10 MIN   40 MIN

STORAGE: **Refrigerate up to 4 days; freeze up to 1 month.**

⅔ cup low-fat Greek yogurt

Juice of ½ lemon

1 garlic clove, grated, or ¼ tsp garlic powder

1 tbsp grated fresh ginger, or ½ tsp ground ginger

1 tsp garam masala, or curry powder

½ tsp paprika

1 tsp salt

½ tsp freshly ground black pepper

½ tsp chili powder (optional)

4 boneless, skinless chicken thighs

For the sandwiches

8 slices white sandwich bread

2 tsp Dijon mustard

1 head butter lettuce, washed and patted dry

2 beefsteak tomatoes, sliced

2 cups shredded red cabbage

A few thin slices of red onion (optional)

Fresh cilantro (optional)

1 In a medium bowl, combine the yogurt, lemon juice, garlic, ginger, garam masala, paprika, salt, pepper, and chili powder, if desired. Add the chicken, and massage for 1 minute. Cover and refrigerate overnight or up to 3 days.

2 Preheat the oven to 400°F (200°C). Line a baking sheet with foil. Place the chicken on the baking sheet, and cook for 35 minutes. Let cool.

3 Spread a thin layer of mustard on 4 slices of bread. Assemble 4 sandwiches, each with 2 to 3 lettuce leaves, sliced tomato, red cabbage, and chicken, as well as red onion and cilantro, if using.

4 Wrap the sandwiches tightly in plastic wrap, and let them sit for 2 to 3 minutes. Cut the sandwiches in half. Remove the plastic wrap before placing the sandwiches in the bento boxes.

SIDE DISH
TOMATO & AVOCADO SALAD

 2 SERVINGS   5 MIN   5 MIN

STORAGE: **Refrigerate up to 1 day.**

1 tbsp freshly squeezed
   lemon juice

½ tsp honey

½ tsp orange marmalade,
   or apricot jam.

5 cherry tomatoes,
   halved, or plum
   tomatoes, quartered

½ avocado, diced

1 In a medium bowl, whisk the lemon juice, honey, and marmalade. Add the tomatoes and avocado and gently toss to combine.

VIETNAMESE LEMONGRASS PORK
WITH FRESH SPRING ROLLS

Sweet, spicy, and aromatic lemongrass pork is paired with fresh shrimp spring rolls bursting with herbs and greens. This bento makes a delightful summer meal or healthy snack box to nibble during the day.

NUTRITION PER BOX

500 calories
Total fat 13g
Cholesterol 123mg
Sodium 600mg
Total carb 36g
Protein 4g

COMPONENTS

MAIN DISH   Vietnamese Lemongrass Pork (page 108)

SIDE DISH   Fresh Spring Rolls (page 109)

GARNISH   cherry tomato, lemon

SERVING TEMPERATURE: spring roll is cold, lemongrass pork is warm or hot

MAIN DISH
VIETNAMESE LEMONGRASS PORK

 4 SERVINGS

 30 MIN

 15 MIN

STORAGE: Refrigerate up to 5 days; freeze up to 30 days.

1lb (450g) pork tenderloin or boneless pork chop, sliced and pounded to about ½ in (1cm) thick

2 tbsp potato starch or corn starch

2 tbsp vegetable oil, divided

1 shallot, finely chopped

1-2 garlic cloves, finely chopped

1 fresh chile, finely chopped (optional)

1 spring onion, finely chopped (optional)

2 tbsp fish sauce

2 tsp water

2 tbsp granulated sugar

For the marinade

1 stalk lemongrass, trimmed and finely chopped

½ tbsp freshly squeezed lime juice

1 tbsp soy sauce

1 In a medium bowl, combine all ingredients for the marinade. Add the pork, and massage the meat to make sure it is fully covered with the marinade. Cover and refrigerate from 20 minutes to overnight.

2 Remove the pork from the marinade. Coat each pork slice with a thin layer of potato starch.

3 In a large nonstick skillet, heat 1 tablespoon oil over medium heat. Add the pork and sear for 1 to 2 minutes on each side. Transfer to a plate and set aside.

4 Scrape any residue from the pan, and return the pan to the stovetop over medium heat. Add the remaining 1 tablespoon oil. When hot, add the shallot, garlic, chile, and spring onion, if using. Cook for 1 to 2 minutes or until aromatic.

5 Add the fish sauce, water, and sugar. When the sauce simmers, add the pork, turning to coat with the sauce. Cook for 1 to 2 minutes or until the sauce has thickened.

SIDE DISH
FRESH SPRING ROLLS

  4 SERVINGS 10 MIN 🔥 10 MIN

STORAGE: **Eat within 4 hours.**

3½oz (100g) rice vermicelli (can also use zoodles, or finely shredded lettuce)

24 large raw shrimp, peeled and deveined, tail off

8 sheets spring roll rice paper

4-5oz (85-110g) lettuce

Fresh herbs, such as Thai basil, sweet basil, mint, cilantro, or scallion

For the dipping sauce

2 tsp fish sauce

2 tsp freshly squeezed lemon juice

4 tsp granulated sugar

5 tbsp water

1 tsp diced fresh chile (optional)

1-2 garlic cloves, grated

1 tbsp roasted peanuts, smashed or coarsely chopped

1. In a medium saucepan, bring 6 cups of water to a boil over high heat. When boiling, add the vermicelli and cook according to package instructions (usually 6–7 minutes). When cooked, remove the noodles and set aside to cool.

2. Bring the remaining water in the saucepan to boil again. Add the shrimp and cook until they become opaque. Frozen shrimp will cook in 2 to 3 minutes; thawed shrimp will cook in 30 seconds. Take out the shrimp and set aside to cool.

3. In a small bowl, whisk together all ingredients for the dipping sauce until the sugar is fully dissolved.

4. To assemble the rolls, place one sheet of rice paper on a clean, dry work surface. Spray each side of the rice paper lightly with water. In the center of the rice paper, place a small pile of vermicelli, lettuce, and herbs. Place three shrimp on top. Roll up the spring roll by bringing in the left, right, and then top sides to the center, and then roll up. Serve with the dipping sauce.

VEGETABLE CURRY
WITH FLATBREAD SALAD WRAPS

Flavorful spices balance the natural sweetness of apple and onion to create a gentle level of heat in this bento meal. Pair the curry with simple flatbread salad wraps, or serve with rice, bread, or udon noodles.

NUTRITION PER BOX

446 calories
Total fat 23g
Cholesterol 186mg
Sodium 602mg
Total Carb 41g
Protein 29g

COMPONENTS

MAIN DISH	Vegetable Curry (page 112)
SIDE DISH	Flatbread Salad Wraps (page 113)
GARNISH	cucumber, black sesame

SERVING TEMPERATURE: salad wraps are cold; curry is hot or warm

MAIN DISH
VEGETABLE CURRY

4–6 SERVINGS   10 MIN   30 MIN

STORAGE: **Refrigerate up to 3 days; freeze up to 30 days.**

2 tsp vegetable oil or olive oil

2 garlic cloves, minced

⅓ yellow onion, sliced

8oz (225g) Impossible Burger or Beyond Beef (or ground beef, pork, turkey, or chicken)

10 mushrooms, diced

1 medium potato, peeled and diced

1 Fuji apple, diced

1 carrot, diced

1 Roma tomato, diced

1 tbsp ground turmeric

1 tbsp paprika

1 tbsp curry powder

2 bay leaves

1 tsp cayenne pepper, or red pepper flakes (optional)

1 tsp mustard seeds (optional)

1 tsp ground coriander (optional)

1 piece Japanese curry block (optional), such as Golden Curry

¼ cup canned light coconut milk

2 tbsp whole-wheat flour

3 tbsp water

1   In a medium saucepan, heat the oil over medium heat. When hot, add the garlic and onion and cook for 2 to 3 minutes. Add the plant-based "meat" and mushrooms, and cook for 2 to 3 minutes more.

2   Add the potato, apple, carrot, tomato, turmeric, paprika, curry powder, and bay leaves, as well as the cayenne, mustard seeds, coriander, and Japanese curry block, if using. Add enough water to the pan to just cover most of the vegetables (1–2 cups). Cover and cook for 20 minutes, stirring occasionally.

3   Add the coconut milk, and simmer for 1 minute. To thicken the sauce, in a small bowl, mix the flour and water. Add the slurry to the pan, stir, and cook for 1 minute or until thickened.

SIDE DISH
FLATBREAD SALAD WRAPS

 4 SERVINGS 3 MIN 5 MIN

STORAGE: **Refrigerate up to 1 day.**

4 pieces flatbread

1 head butter lettuce

4-8 beefsteak tomato slices

¼ red onion, sliced

4 hard-boiled eggs, sliced

1 Cut each flatbread in half. Wrap each piece of flatbread around a few lettuce leaves, 1 to 2 tomato slices, a few slices of red onion, and sliced hard-boiled egg. Use a piece of raw spaghetti or a toothpick to secure the flatbread if needed.

WESTERN-STYLE BENTO

HONEY MUSTARD SALMON WITH CURRIED CAULIFLOWER AND SPICY KALE

Broiling gives the sweet and tangy sauce on this salmon a beautiful glaze, and the spicy, pungent flavors of the side dishes balance the sweetness of the honey mustard.

NUTRITION PER BOX

474 Calories
Total fat 22g
Cholesterol 72mg
Sodium 1,115mg
Total carb 34g
Protein 37g

COMPONENTS

MAIN DISH   Honey Mustard Salmon (page 118)

SIDE DISHES   Curried Cauliflower (page 119)
Spicy Kale (page 119)

STAPLE   Quinoa Rice (page 154; ⅓ cup per serving)

GARNISH   cherry tomato

SERVING TEMPERATURE: hot or warm

MAIN DISH
HONEY MUSTARD SALMON

 4 SERVINGS   5 MIN   10 MIN

STORAGE: Refrigerate up to 3 days; freeze up to 30 days.

1 tbsp olive oil

1 tbsp Dijon mustard

1 tbsp honey

1 tsp soy sauce

4 salmon fillets, each about 5oz (150g) and 1-in (2.5cm) thick

Juice of ½ lemon

1 Adjust an oven rack to sit about 3 to 4 inches (7.5–10cm) from the broiler, and preheat the broiler. Line a baking sheet with foil, and grease lightly with oil. In a small bowl, mix the olive oil, mustard, honey, and soy sauce.

2 Pat the salmon dry with paper towels or a clean dish towel. Place the salmon on the prepared baking sheet, skin side down. Pour the honey mustard sauce evenly over each fillet.

3 Broil on high for 8 to 10 minutes. The broiler can easily char the surface, so check frequently after 8 minutes. The glaze should be bubbling and beginning to brown but not blackened. Squeeze lemon juice over top before serving.

SIDE DISHES
CURRIED CAULIFLOWER

4 SERVINGS   5 MIN   25 MIN

STORAGE: **Refrigerate up to 3 days.**

1½ tbsp olive oil

½ tbsp ghee, butter, or olive oil

½ tsp curry powder

½ tsp ground turmeric

½ tsp paprika

½ tsp ground coriander

1 tsp salt

4 cups bite-sized cauliflower florets

Juice of ½ lemon

Chopped fresh parsley (optional), to garnish

1 Preheat the oven to 450°F (230°C). Line a baking sheet with foil or parchment paper.

2 In a large bowl, stir together the olive oil, ghee, curry powder, turmeric, paprika, coriander, and salt. Add the cauliflower and toss to coat.

3 Spread the cauliflower on the prepared baking sheet. Roast for 20 minutes. Remove from the oven, and squeeze lemon juice over top. Garnish with parsley, if using.

SPICY KALE

4 SERVINGS   5 MIN   10 MIN

STORAGE: **Refrigerate up to 3 days.**

1 tbsp olive oil or vegetable oil

2 garlic cloves, minced, or ½ tsp garlic powder

5-6 dried red chiles, broken into halves, or ½ tsp red pepper flakes

5-6 mushrooms, cut into quarters

1 bunch of kale, stems removed, chopped, about 5oz

2 tsp soy sauce

Pinch of salt

1 In a large nonstick skillet, heat the oil over medium heat. Add the garlic and chiles, and cook for 1 to 2 minutes until the garlic is slightly browned. Add the mushrooms, and cook for 1 to 2 minutes more.

2 Add the kale, soy sauce, and salt. Increase the heat to medium-high, and cook for 2 to 3 minutes, stirring frequently until the kale is dark green and cooked.

PESTO COD PARCEL WITH SAUTÉED ZUCCHINI & MUSHROOMS

A tidy package loaded with Mediterranean fresh fragrance, this bento brings to mind the joy of opening a gift from abroad.

Don't forget to pack some bread with this bento—the sauce from the pesto and tomatoes is the real essence here.

COMPONENTS

MAIN DISH   Pesto Cod Parcel (page 122)

SIDE DISH   Sautéed Zucchini & Mushrooms (page 123)

STAPLE   French bread (½ slice per serving)

SERVING TEMPERATURE: hot or warm

MAIN DISH
PESTO COD PARCEL

 4 SERVINGS   5 MIN   15 MIN

STORAGE: **Refrigerate up to 3 days.**

4 cod fillets, each about 5oz (150g)

4 tbsp pesto

1 cup cherry tomatoes, halved

4 sprigs fresh rosemary, or 2 tsp dried rosemary

Salt and freshly ground black pepper, to taste

1 Preheat the oven to 400°F (200°C). Prepare four sheets of parchment paper, each about 12 x 15 inches (30 x 38cm).

2 Pat dry the fish, and place each fillet in the center of one piece of parchment. On each fillet, spread 1 tablespoon of pesto, followed by ¼ cup cherry tomatoes and 1 rosemary sprig. Sprinkle each fillet with salt and pepper.

3 To seal the packets, fold the parchment lengthwise up and over the fish. Beginning at one edge, make small folds all the way around to create a sealed packet.

4 Place the packets on a baking sheet and bake for 10 minutes. When opening the packet, be careful of the steam. When reheating, make sure that the packet is completely sealed.

SIDE DISH
SAUTÉED ZUCCHINI & MUSHROOMS

  4 SERVINGS   5 MIN   10 MIN

STORAGE: **Refrigerate up to 3 days.**

1 tbsp olive oil or
 vegetable oil

2 garlic cloves, grated,
 or ¼ tsp garlic powder

2 tsp herbes de Provence,
 or another blend of dried
 herbs

½ cup diced red onion

½ tsp red pepper flakes
 (optional)

2 cups diced mushrooms

4 cups diced zucchini

Salt and freshly ground
 black pepper, to taste

1 In a large nonstick skillet, heat the oil over medium heat. Add the garlic, herbes de Provence, onion, and red pepper flakes, if using. Sauté for 1 to 2 minutes or until the onion is soft. Add the mushrooms and zucchini. Sauté for 4 to 5 minutes, stirring occasionally. Season with salt and pepper, to taste.

PARMESAN CHICKEN
WITH SAUTÉED BRUSSELS SPROUTS AND SAUSAGE RIGATONI

This bento is perfect for the holiday season or anytime you crave warming comfort food. Tender chicken is baked with a crisp bread crumb coating and paired with hearty rigatoni and savory Brussels sprouts.

NUTRITION PER BOX

497 calories
Total fat 23g
Cholesterol 84mg
Sodium 810mg
Total carb 44g
Protein 36g

COMPONENTS

MAIN DISH	Parmesan Chicken (page 126)
SIDE DISHES	Sautéed Brussels Sprouts (page 127)
	Sausage Rigatoni (page 127)
GARNISH	fresh rosemary

SERVING TEMPERATURE: hot or warm

MAIN DISH
PARMESAN CHICKEN

 4 SERVINGS   10 MIN   20 MIN

STORAGE: **Refrigerate up to 4 days; freeze up to 30 days.**

3 boneless, skinless chicken thighs, each cut into 3–4 bite-sized pieces

Dash of salt

Dash of freshly ground black pepper

For the seasoned bread crumbs

6 tbsp panko bread crumbs

3 tbsp finely grated Parmesan cheese

3 tbsp olive oil

¼ tsp salt

1 garlic clove, minced, or 1 tsp garlic powder

½ tsp dried oregano

½ tsp dried rosemary

Pinch of freshly ground black pepper

1   Preheat the oven to 400°F (200°C). Line a baking sheet with foil. In a small bowl, mix all of the ingredients for the seasoned bread crumbs until well combined.

2   Lightly season the chicken with salt and pepper. Arrange the chicken on the prepared baking sheet, and spread the seasoned bread crumbs over each piece of chicken. Bake for 15 minutes, and then broil for 2 to 3 minutes or until the bread crumbs are golden brown.

SIDE DISHES
SAUTÉED BRUSSELS SPROUTS

 4 SERVINGS   10 MIN   15 MIN

STORAGE: Refrigerate up to 4 days.

2 tsp olive oil or vegetable oil

1 garlic clove, minced, or a pinch of garlic powder

1 cup quartered mushrooms

1 tsp dried parsley

Dash of red pepper flakes (optional)

1lb (450g) Brussels sprouts, trimmed and halved

1 tsp soy sauce

Pinch of salt

⅓ cup hot water

1 In a large nonstick skillet, heat the oil over medium heat. Add the garlic, mushrooms, parsley, and red pepper flakes, if using. Cook for 1 to 2 minutes.

2 Add the Brussels sprouts, soy sauce, and salt. Sauté for 3 to 4 minutes. Add water and cover. Cook over medium-high heat for 2 to 3 minutes. Remove the lid and cook for 2 to 3 minutes, or until the Brussels sprouts are bright green and tender.

SAUSAGE RIGATONI

 4 SERVINGS   5 MIN   15 MIN

STORAGE: Refrigerate up to 4 days.

2 cups uncooked rigatoni

2 tsp olive oil or vegetable oil

2 anchovies

Pinch of garlic powder

1 tsp dried parsley or Italian seasoning blend

Dash of red pepper flakes (optional)

2 precooked Italian chicken sausages, sliced

1 red bell pepper, diced

2 tbsp tomato paste or 4 tbsp tomato sauce

Pinch of salt

1 In a large pot, bring 6 cups of salted water to a boil. Add the rigatoni, and boil for 10 minutes. Reserve 1 cup pasta water before draining.

2 While the pasta cooks, in a large nonstick skillet, heat the oil over medium heat. Add the anchovies, garlic powder, parsley, red pepper flakes (if using), and sliced sausage. Cook for 2 minutes, stirring occasionally, until the sausage is lightly browned and the anchovies have broken down.

3 Stir in the red bell pepper and tomato paste. Cook for 3 to 4 minutes. Add ⅔ cup to 1 cup reserved pasta water to thin the sauce. (If using tomato sauce, ⅓–½ cup is enough.)

4 Reduce the heat to low, and stir in the rigatoni. Adjust the density of the sauce by adding more reserved pasta water, if needed. Add salt to taste.

MEATBALLS
WITH TOMATO SAUCE AND
SPINACH MUSHROOM GNOCCHI

This cozy Italian-inspired bento is ideal for cooler fall or winter weather. Savory meatballs with a simple homemade tomato sauce are the perfect accompaniment to creamy and comforting gnocchi.

NUTRITION PER BOX

499 calories
Total fat 21g
Cholesterol 177mg
Sodium 1,930mg
Total carb 45g
Protein 34g

COMPONENTS

MAIN DISH   Meatballs with Tomato Sauce (page 130)

SIDE DISH   Spinach Mushroom Gnocchi (page 131)

GARNISH   cherry tomato, fresh rosemary

SERVING TEMPERATURE: hot or warm

MAIN DISH
MEATBALLS
WITH TOMATO SAUCE

 4 SERVINGS   10 MIN   25 MIN

STORAGE: Refrigerate up to 5 days;
freeze up to 30 days.

For meatballs

½ cup panko bread crumbs

⅓ cup milk

1lb (450g) ground turkey or other ground meat

2 eggs

1 tsp Italian seasoning blend

1 garlic clove, grated, or a pinch of garlic powder

1 tbsp grated Parmesan cheese

1 tsp salt

½ tsp freshly ground black pepper

For the sauce

1½ tsp olive oil

¼ yellow onion, diced

1½ cups diced fresh tomato

1 tsp Italian seasoning blend

2 tbsp tomato paste

1½ cups low-sodium vegetable stock

1 tsp salt

2 bay leaves

1   To make the meatballs, in a large bowl, soak the bread crumbs with milk for 1 to 2 minutes. Add the remaining ingredients for the meatballs. Using your hands, combine the ingredients until the mixture is fully combined, and shape into meatballs about 1½ inches (4cm) in diameter. Arrange the meatballs on a baking sheet, and place in the freezer to set. Preheat the oven to 450°F (230°C).

2   Meanwhile, make the sauce. In a medium pot, heat the oil over medium heat. Add the onion, tomato, and Italian seasoning. Cook for 3 to 5 minutes until the tomato is soft. Add the tomato paste, vegetable stock, salt, and bay leaves. Cook for 5 minutes, stirring occasionally. Reduce the heat to low.

3   When the oven is preheated, remove the meatballs from the freezer, and bake them for 10 to 12 minutes. After baking, broil them on high for 2 to 3 minutes or until golden brown. Add the meatballs to the tomato sauce.

SIDE DISH
SPINACH MUSHROOM GNOCCHI

4 SERVINGS   10 MIN   10 MIN

STORAGE: **Refrigerate up to 3 days.**

2 cups mini gnocchi

1 tbsp olive oil

1 tsp butter

2 garlic cloves, diced, or ¼ tsp garlic powder

1 cup sliced mushrooms

12oz (340g) baby spinach, chopped

½ tsp salt

Dash of freshly grated black pepper

Grated Parmesan cheese, to serve

1 Prepare the gnocchi according to the package instructions.

2 While the gnocchi is boiling, in a large nonstick skillet, heat the oil and butter over medium heat. Add the garlic and mushrooms, and cook for 2 to 3 minutes until the mushrooms are soft. Add the spinach and salt, and then increase the heat to high. Stir frequently for 1 to 2 minutes until the spinach is soft.

3 When the gnocchi is done, reserve a few tablespoons of cooking water. Drain the gnocchi and add it to the skillet. Cook over medium heat for 1 to 2 minutes, and add a few tablespoons of reserved cooking water to create a light sauce. Sprinkle with pepper and Parmesan cheese before serving.

SPICY KALE & GROUND BEEF WITH TOMATO SCRAMBLED EGGS AND KABOCHA PUMPKIN BALL

NUTRITION PER BOX

271 calories
Total fat 19g
Cholesterol 181mg
Sodium 704mg
Total carb 8g
Protein 19g

This special Halloween bento is brimming with flavorful vegetables and sweet autumn kabocha pumpkin balls. Get creative and decorate your bento with seaweed sheets to make it extra spooky.

COMPONENTS

MAIN DISH	Spicy Kale & Ground Beef (page 134)
SIDE DISHES	Tomato Scrambled Eggs (page 135)
	Kabocha Pumpkin Balls (page 135)
GARNISH	sesame seeds

SERVING TEMPERATURE: hot or warm

MAIN DISH
SPICY KALE & GROUND BEEF

 4 SERVINGS   5 MIN   10 MIN

STORAGE: **Refrigerate up to 3 days.**

1 bunch of kale

1 tbsp vegetable oil

2 garlic cloves, minced, or ½ tsp garlic powder

8oz (225g) ground beef, or other ground meat

1 tsp oyster sauce, or thick soy sauce (soy paste)

1 tbsp harissa, or gochujang (Korean chili paste)

Pinch of salt

1 Remove the kale stems, and chop the kale leaves into bite-sized pieces. Wash and dry the kale, and set aside.

2 In a large nonstick skillet, heat the oil over medium heat. When hot, add the garlic and cook for 1 to 2 minutes. Add the ground beef, oyster sauce, and harissa, and sauté for 2 to 3 minutes until the meat is fully cooked.

3 Push the meat to the sides of the pan. Add the kale and a pinch of salt. Increase the heat to medium-high heat, and cook, stirring frequently, for 2 to 3 minutes or until the kale turns dark green.

SIDE DISHES
TOMATO SCRAMBLED EGGS

 4 SERVINGS   5 MIN   10 MIN

STORAGE: **Refrigerate up to 3 days.**

3 large eggs

½ tsp salt

2 tbsp vegetable oil

1 spring onion, or
  2 scallions, finely
  chopped (optional)

2 cups diced fresh
  tomatoes

1 tbsp tomato sauce or
  1 tsp tomato paste

2 tbsp water

1 tsp soy sauce

½ tsp granulated sugar

1 In a small bowl, whisk the eggs and salt. In a large nonstick skillet, heat the oil over medium heat. Add the eggs and wait for 10 seconds. Use a spatula to push the egg from the edges to the center, and then cook for 60 to 90 seconds, using the spatula to break up the egg. When the egg is about half cooked, transfer to a plate and set aside.

2 In the same pan, sauté half of the spring onion, if using. Add the tomato and cook for 2 to 3 minutes or until the tomato is soft. Add the tomato sauce, water, soy sauce, sugar, and a pinch of salt. Cook for 1 to 2 minutes or until the sauce has thickened.

3 Remove from the heat. Add the scrambled eggs and mix them with the sauce. Garnish with the remaining spring onion, if using.

- -

KABOCHA PUMPKIN BALLS

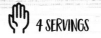 4 SERVINGS   5 MIN   5 MIN

STORAGE: **Refrigerate up to 3 days.**

½ kabocha squash
  (Japanese pumpkin)

1 tbsp butter, melted

½ tsp maple syrup

Pinch of salt

Pinch of ground cinnamon

Nori seaweed sheet
  (optional), for decoration

1 Microwave the squash for 2 to 3 minutes. (This will make it easier to remove the flesh.) Scrape out the seeds and discard. Using a spoon, scoop out the flesh of the squash. If the flesh is still hard, microwave it for 1 to 2 minutes more.

2 In a medium bowl, mix the squash with the butter, maple syrup, salt, and cinnamon until the mixture is smooth. Spread a piece of plastic wrap on your work surface. Place 2 to 3 tablespoons of the mixture in the center of the plastic wrap, gather the four corners of the plastic wrap, and shape the mixture into a ball. Repeat with the rest of the mixture. Remove the plastic wrap before packing the balls into your bento boxes. If you feel playful, cut a jack-o'-lantern face from a nori seaweed sheet to decorate the balls.

Spicy Kale & Ground Beef **135**

CUMIN LAMB KEBABS
WITH UYGHUR RICE PILAF

Drawing on the culinary tradition of Uyghur street food in western China, these lamb kebabs have an irresistable flavor and aroma thanks to a spice blend of cumin, paprika, and garlic. They can be baked or grilled.

NUTRITION PER BOX

450 calories
Total fat 22g
Cholesterol 58mg
Sodium 990mg
Total carb 43g
Protein 4g

COMPONENTS

MAIN DISH   Cumin Lamb Kebabs (page 138)

SIDE DISH   Uyghur Rice Pilaf (page 139)

SERVING TEMPERATURE: hot or warm

MAIN DISH
CUMIN LAMB KEBABS

 8 SERVINGS 30 MIN 15 MIN

STORAGE: **Refrigerate up to 5 days.**

2lb (1kg) boneless leg of lamb, cut into bite-sized pieces

½ zucchini, sliced

¼ red onion, sliced

½ red bell pepper, diced

½ yellow bell pepper, diced

1 tbsp vegetable oil

½ tsp salt

Dash of ground cumin

Dash of paprika

For the rub

2 tsp ground cumin

2 tsp paprika

2 tsp chili powder

1 tsp ground Szechuan pepper

2 tsp salt

2 garlic cloves, grated, or ¼ tsp garlic powder

2 tbsp vegetable oil

1 tsp baking soda

1 In a medium bowl, combine all ingredients for the rub. Add the lamb, and use your hands to coat the meat fully in the spice mixture. Cover and refrigerate for at least 20 minutes or overnight. (It will become more flavorful the longer it sits.)

2 Preheat the oven to 425°F (215°C). In a medium bowl, toss the zucchini, onion, and peppers with the oil and salt. Spread them in a roasting pan and place the lamb on top of the vegetables. (If you prefer skewers, skewer the lamb and vegetables together, and then spread the skewers on a roasting pan.)

3 Roast for 10 to 12 minutes, and then broil for 1 to 2 minutes to char the lamb. Sprinkle with cumin and paprika before serving. (Save the drippings from the roasting pan for the pilaf.)

SIDE DISH
UYGHUR RICE PILAF

 8 SERVINGS   10 MIN   30 MIN

STORAGE: **Refrigerate up to 4 days.**

2 tbsp vegetable oil

1 cup julienned carrots

1 cup sliced onion

8oz (225g) lamb, diced or minced (optional, can be replaced with drippings from roast lamb)

1 tsp ground cumin

1 tsp paprika

1 tsp salt

½ tsp freshly ground black pepper

2 cups basmati rice, rinsed and drained

4 cups water

Raisins, to garnish

Crushed almonds (optional), to garnish

1 In a Dutch oven or large saucepan, heat the oil over medium heat. When hot, add the carrots and onion. Cook for 2 to 3 minutes or until soft. Add the lamb, cumin, paprika, salt, and pepper. Cook for 2 to 3 minutes.

2 Stir in the rice. Add the water and bring to a simmer. Reduce the heat to medium-low and cover. Cook for 12 minutes or until the water has absorbed. Remove from the heat and let rest, covered, for 10 minutes. Sprinkle with raisins and crushed almonds, if using, before serving.

ROASTED HARISSA CHICKEN WITH
CHARD & CHICKPEA STIR-FRY

Marinated with traditional Tunisian harissa paste, harissa chicken is a flavor bomb with the aroma of smoked pepper and mild spiciness. If you prefer less heat, add the optional miso and sugar.

COMPONENTS

MAIN DISH Roasted Harissa Chicken (page 142)

SIDE DISH Chard & Chickpea Stir-Fry (page 143)

STAPLE Jasmine Rice (page 153; 1/3 cup per serving)

GARNISH cherry tomato, lemon

SERVING TEMPERATURE: hot or warm

MAIN DISH
ROASTED HARISSA CHICKEN

 4 SERVINGS 25 MIN 20 MIN

STORAGE: Refrigerate up to 5 days; freeze up to 30 days.

4 boneless, skinless chicken thighs

1 tbsp freshly squeezed lemon juice

For the marinade

3 tbsp harissa

1 tbsp olive oil

½ tsp paprika

½ tsp coriander seeds (optional)

1 tbsp miso (optional, to reduce heat)

1 tsp granulated sugar (optional, to reduce heat)

1 Preheat the oven to 450°F (230°C). Line a baking sheet with foil or parchment paper.

2 In a small bowl, whisk together the marinade ingredients. (For a milder version, add the optional miso and sugar to reduce the heat but still enjoy the flavor of harissa.) Add the chicken, turning to fully coat. Cover and refrigerate for at least 20 minutes.

3 Place the chicken on the prepared baking sheet. Roast for 15 minutes, and then broil for 2 to 3 minutes. Drizzle the lemon juice over top before serving.

SIDE DISH
CHARD & CHICKPEA STIR-FRY

 4 SERVINGS 10 MIN 8 MIN

STORAGE: **Refrigerate up to 3 days.**

2 bunches of rainbow Swiss chard

1 tbsp olive oil

4 garlic cloves, minced, or ½ tsp garlic powder

½ tsp paprika

1 cup canned chickpeas, drained and rinsed

Pinch of salt

3 tbsp chopped sun-dried tomatoes (packed in oil)

1 tbsp freshly squeezed lemon juice

1 Cut the chard stems into 1-inch (2.5cm) pieces and the leaves into bite-sized pieces. Keep the stems and leaves separate.

2 In a large nonstick skillet, heat the oil over medium heat. Add the garlic, paprika, chickpeas, chard stems, and salt. Cook for 2 to 3 minutes until the chard is soft. Stir in the sun-dried tomatoes.

3 Push the vegetables to the edges of the pan, and increase the heat to high. Add the chard leaves to the pan, and cook, stirring frequently, until the leaves are soft. Season with salt to taste, and drizzle the lemon juice over top.

BALSAMIC PORK
WITH GARLIC ASPARAGUS AND TUNA-STUFFED TOMATO

Balsamic vinegar is reduced to a dark, rich glaze, resulting in a flavorful sweet and sour dish that's a perfect match for the fresh asparagus and lovely tuna-stuffed tomato.

NUTRITION PER BOX

500 calories
Total fat 22g
Cholesterol 25mg
Sodium 1,325mg
Total carb 45g
Protein 42g

COMPONENTS

MAIN DISH	Balsamic Pork (page 146)
SIDE DISHES	Garlic Asparagus (page 147)
	Tuna-Stuffed Tomato (page 147)
STAPLE	Jasmine Rice (page 153; 1/3 cup per serving)
GARNISH	lemon, radish

SERVING TEMPERATURE: hot or warm

MAIN DISH
BALSAMIC PORK

 4 SERVINGS   5 MIN   15 MIN

STORAGE: **Refrigerate up to 5 days; freeze up to 30 days.**

1lb (450g) pork tenderloin, sliced into medallions and pounded to ½-in (1cm) thick

2 tbsp all-purpose flour

1 tbsp vegetable oil

2 tbsp butter

1 tsp salt

⅓ cup balsamic vinegar

1 tbsp granulated sugar

1 Coat the pork with a thin layer of flour on both sides, and shake off the excess flour.

2 In a large nonstick skillet, heat the oil and melt the butter over medium-low heat. When hot, add the pork. Sprinkle with salt, and cook for 2 to 3 minutes on each side. (If your pan cannot fit in all the pork at one time, use half of the butter in the first batch, and melt the remaining butter before cooking the second batch.)

3 Add the vinegar and sugar. Bring to boil and cook until the sauce has thickened.

SIDE DISHES
GARLIC ASPARAGUS

 4 SERVINGS   5 MIN   10 MIN

STORAGE: **Refrigerate up to 4 days.**

2 tsp olive oil

2 garlic cloves, minced,
or ¼ tsp garlic powder

1 bunch of asparagus,
trimmed and cut into 2-in
(5cm) pieces

½ tsp salt

Dash of freshly ground
black pepper

1 tsp freshly squeezed
lemon juice

1 In a large nonstick skillet, heat the oil over medium-low heat. Add the garlic and cook for 2 to 3 minutes until golden brown. Add the asparagus, and increase the heat to high. Cook, stirring frequently, for 3 to 4 minutes until the asparagus is tender. Season with salt, pepper, and lemon juice.

TUNA-STUFFED
TOMATO

 4 SERVINGS   10 MIN   15 MIN

STORAGE: **Refrigerate up to 4 days.**

4 medium vine-ripe
tomatoes

Salt and freshly ground
black pepper, to taste

1 (5oz; 142g) can tuna,
drained

3 tbsp corn kernels (fresh,
canned, or frozen)

3 tbsp panko bread
crumbs

1 tbsp crushed walnuts
(optional)

2 tbsp Dijon mustard

2 tbsp shredded
mozzarella or cheddar
cheese

1 Preheat the oven to 400°F (200°C). Slice of the top of each tomato, and scoop out the pulp. (It can be frozen and used in pasta or soup. Don't waste it!) Sprinkle salt and pepper into the tomato and on the tomato tops.

2 In a medium bowl, mix together the tuna, corn, bread crumbs, walnuts (if using), and mustard. Season with salt and pepper to taste. Fill each tomato with the tuna mixture, and sprinkle the mozzarella over top.

3 Place the stuffed tomatoes and tomato tops in a small baking dish. Roast for 12 to 15 minutes or until golden brown.

ROASTED PORTOBELLO BURGER

WITH SPICY KOREAN COLESLAW

Make a yummy vegetarian meal from your pantry inventory and with minimum effort. Enjoy this healthy burger with aromatic coleslaw as a meat-free treat to yourself. Don't forget to separate the coleslaw from the burger to keep the bun dry.

COMPONENTS

MAIN DISH   Roasted Portobello Burger (page 150)

SIDE DISH   Spicy Korean Coleslaw (page 151)

GARNISH   apple slices, cherry tomato

SERVING TEMPERATURE: burger is warm, coleslaw is cold

MAIN DISH
ROASTED PORTOBELLO BURGER

 4 SERVINGS 10 MIN 25 MIN

STORAGE: Refrigerate up to 4 days.

4 portobello mushrooms

5-6 tbsp pesto

2 tbsp chopped
  sun-dried tomatoes

Pinch of salt and freshly
  ground black pepper

Truffle oil (optional)

Hot sauce or sriracha
  (optional)

4 tsp shredded
  mozzarella cheese

To assemble

4 eggs

4 hamburger buns

2 tsp butter or
  mayonnaise

8 lettuce leaves

4 slices tomato

Red onion slices
  (optional), or Pickled
  Onion (page 39)

1 Preheat the oven to 350°F (175°C). Cut the stems from the mushrooms and dice the stems, keeping the caps intact.

2 Spread the pesto on the inner side of the mushroom caps, and then add some of the sun-dried tomatoes and diced stems to each cap. Sprinkle with salt and pepper, as well as truffle oil and hot sauce, if using. Sprinkle with mozzarella.

3 Place the mushrooms on a baking sheet, and roast for 25 minutes. Check after 15 minutes, and cover with foil if the cheese is browned.

4 While the mushrooms roast, fry the eggs according to your preference.

5 Spread butter or mayonnaise on the buns, and assemble the burgers with lettuce, tomato, onion, portobello mushroom, and fried egg.

SIDE DISH
SPICY KOREAN
COLESLAW

 4 SERVINGS   10 MIN   5 MIN

STORAGE: **Refrigerate up to 3 days.**

3 cups thinly sliced green cabbage, drained

1 cup thinly sliced red cabbage, drained (or can be replaced by green cabbage)

1 scallion, thinly sliced

For the dressing

1 tbsp gochujang (Korean chili paste)

2 tbsp sesame oil

2 tbsp olive oil

3 tbsp rice vinegar or apple cider vinegar

1 tsp soy sauce

2–3 tbsp granulated sugar, to taste

Pinch of salt

For the crunchy topping (optional)

2 tbsp toasted sesame seeds

½ cup chopped pecans

½ cup crumbled dry ramen noodles

1 In a medium bowl, combine all dressing ingredients. Add the green and red cabbage and scallions, and toss until fully coated.

2 To prepare the optional crunchy topping, mix together all ingredients and sprinkle over coleslaw before serving.

STAPLES

JASMINE RICE
(STOVETOP)

 6 CUPS   3 MIN   20 MIN

STORAGE: Refrigerate up to 5 days; freeze up to 30 days.

3 cups water

2 cups white jasmine
rice, rinsed 3 times and
drained

½ tsp salt

1 tsp olive oil

1 In a medium saucepan, bring the water to a boil over high heat. Stir in the rice, salt, and oil. When the water begins boiling again, cover with a lid, and reduce the heat to low. Cook, covered, for 15 minutes.

2 Check for doneness by squeezing one grain of rice between your fingers; it should flatten easily. Cooked jasmine rice is fluffy, dry, and al dente in texture. If it's too hard, add 2 to 3 tablespoons water and cook, covered, for 5 minutes more. Fluff with a fork when done.

BASMATI RICE
(STOVETOP)

 6 CUPS   35 MIN   10 MIN

STORAGE: Refrigerate up to 5 days; freeze up to 30 days.

2 cups basmati rice,
rinsed 3 times

4 cups water

½ tsp salt

1 tsp olive oil

1 In a medium bowl, soak the rice in water for 30 minutes, and then drain it.

2 In a medium saucepan, bring the water to a boil over high heat. When boiling, stir in the rice, salt, and oil. Boil for 6 minutes. Check for doneness by squeezing one grain of rice between your fingers. Cooked basmati rice is fluffy, soft, and each grain of rice can be separated easily. If it's still too hard, boil for 30 seconds more.

3 Drain the rice, and use a fork to fluff it. If the rice feels too soft, rinse it with cold water and drain again.

MEDIUM- OR SHORT-GRAIN WHITE RICE
(STOVETOP)

 6 CUPS   25 MIN   🔥 30 MIN

STORAGE: **Refrigerate up to 5 days; freeze up to 30 days.**

2 cups medium- or short-grain rice, rinsed 3 times

2 cups water

1 In a medium bowl, soak the rice in water for 20 to 25 minutes until the rice becomes opaque, and then drain the rice.

2 In a medium saucepan, combine the rice with 2 cups water and bring to boil over high heat.

3 Stir the rice quickly to make sure it does not stick to the bottom of the pan. Reduce the heat to low, and cover with a lid. Cook for 10 minutes. (Do not lift the lid while cooking.)

4 Remove the pan from the heat and let sit, covered, for 15 minutes. Check for doneness by squeezing one grain of rice between your fingers. Cooked rice should be sticky and al dente.

Variations

For Purple Rice: Use 1¾ cups medium- or short-grain white rice and ¼ cup black rice. Cook as directed.

For Quinoa Rice: Use 1¾ cups medium- or short-grain white rice and ¼ cup quinoa (tri-color or red quinoa preferred). Cook as directed.

MULTICOOKER RICE

 6 CUPS   5 MIN   25 MIN

STORAGE: Refrigerate up to 5 days; freeze up to 30 days.

2 cups rice (any variety),
   rinsed 3 times

2 cups water

1 tsp olive oil

1 Place the rice, water, and oil in the multicooker. Set to Pressure Cook (High) for 4 minutes.

2 When the cook time is done, allow the pressure to release naturally for 10 minutes, and then quick release the remaining pressure. Fluff with a fork and serve.

Variations

Replace up to ¼ the rice with another grain such as quinoa, black rice, or brown rice.

For more flavor and nutrients, add diced vegetables to the rice before cooking. Popular options include sweet potato, Murasaki sweet potato, chestnuts, tomato, or kabocha squash. Peel and cut any vegetable additions into bite-sized pieces, up to 2 cups. Place them on top of the rice in the multicooker before cooking. Cook as directed. After cooking, mix the vegetables into the rice, or take them out and enjoy them separately.

INDEX

ACKNOWLEDGMENTS

I want to thank my dear partner, Ian, for all the love and support that encouraged me through the process of writing this book. Special thanks to my best consulting team: Jean, Claudia, Crystal, and Chia-Ning for always answering my phone calls and discussing recipes with me. I'd also like to express my gratitude to my parents, my aunt, Se-yan, Chi, Brook, Leticia, Olivia, and Brad for kindly offering me help and materials that are used in this book. Last but not least, I really appreciate my editor, Ann, for her excellent work and contributions to this book.

ABOUT THE AUTHOR

Ophelia Chien is an avid cook and the creator of Vanilla Infinite, an Instagram account where she shares her colorful bento box creations. Originally from Taiwan, she currently lives in the San Francisco Bay area while pursuing her MBA.